Building the BEST VERSION of You

By

Harris Kern and A'ishah Khan

Building the BEST VERSION of You

Café con Leche

By

Harris Kern and A'ishah Khan

Building the Best Version of You

© Copyright 2021, Harris Kern and A'ishah Khan

ISBN: 978-1-7370614-2-7

All rights reserved. No part of this publication may be reproduced, stored in a retrieval system, or transmitted in any form or by any means—electronic, mechanical, photo-copy, recording, or any other—except for brief quotations in printed reviews, without the prior written consent of the author.

Published by

3 Griffin Hill Court
The Woodlands, TX. 77382
281-465-0119
www.cafeconlechebooks.com

Table of Contents

FOREWORD	**IX**
○ Society Says . . .	ix
PREFACE	**XIII**
INTRODUCTION	**1**
○ How it Started for Me	3
○ Why I Wrote This Book	4
○ You Have the Power	5
○ What to Expect—Visualize a New You	12
○ Why These Ten Principles	15
○ Let's Get Ready to Start	16
CHAPTER 1: TRAINING YOUR MIND	**19**
○ How to Train Your Mind	20
○ Assess Your Past Performance…Be Brutally Honest	22
○ Treating Every Day Equally	28
○ Establish Phrases—Play Mind Games	31
• *Phrases and Tips to Help You Exercise Consistently*	*33*
• *Phrases and Tips to Help You Prevent Goal Failure*	*34*
○ Set an Expiration Date and Live Life with Urgency	35
○ Conclusion—Straight from Yoda's Mouth	38

CHAPTER 2: DEVELOP YOUR EMOTIONAL QUOTIENT (EQ) 41
- EQ Defined 42
- The Three Categories of EQ 44
- How to Improve Your EQ 46
- Learning to Forgive Yourself 47
- Keep Your Cool—Manage Your Emotions 48
  - *Thirteen Tips on How to Develop Your EQ 48*
- Possess an Even-Keel Demeanor—Plan for the Worst 52
- Redirecting Negative Emotions 54
- Working with Difficult People 57
- Conflict Management—Influencing Others in the Right Direction 61
  - *Nine Tips on How to Influence People 61*
- It's How You Communicate 64
  - *Fourteen Tips on How to Communicate Effectively 65*
- An EQ Case Study: The Doctor and His Two Sons 69
- Transfer Your Emotions and Free Your Mind 73
- Conclusion—EQ is MUCH More Important Than Your IQ 74

CHAPTER 3: ATTAINING YOUR GOALS 77
- The Four Priorities of Life 79
- Goal Setting and Goal Management 81
  - *Ten Tips for Setting Goals 81*
  - *Seven Tips for Managing Your Goals 88*
- Maintaining Balance 90
  - *A Cautionary Tale Straight from the Horse's Mouth 91*
- Conclusion—Fulfill Your Dreams 92

CHAPTER 4: TIME MANAGEMENT 95
- How to Not Waste Time 96
- Live a Structured Lifestyle 97
  - *Establish and Follow a To-Do List 98*
  - *Adhere to an AM and PM Routine 99*
  - *Be Organized 103*
- You're Running out of Time—Manage Yourself 104
  - *Seven Tips on How to Manage Yourself to Utilize Time Efficiently 105*

- Technology Alert: All Circuits are Busy 109
  - *Nine Tips of how to Overcome Technology Addiction* *111*
- Conclusion—If We Only Had a Time Machine 113

CHAPTER 5: MANAGE YOUR SLEEP 115

- Manage it or sleep your life away 116
  - *Nine Tips on How to Manage Your Sleep* *121*
- Conclusion—Sleep Right—Sleep Tight—Accomplish More 133

CHAPTER 6: FOCUS ON YOUR FINANCES... 135

- The World Revolves Around Money..136
  - *Fifteen Tips to Financial Freedom*...*138*
- Conclusion—Manage Your Money or Else Pay a Hefty Price 149

CHAPTER 7: EXCEL IN YOUR CAREER AND/OR BUSINESS 151

- Jobs, Careers and Businesses 151
  - *Thirteen Tips on How to Excel in Your Career*..*152*
  - *Nine Tips on How to Build a Startup Business While Working a 9 to 5 Job* *165*
- Conclusion—It's Your Livelihood—Make it Worthwhile......................168

CHAPTER 8: MANAGE YOUR RELATIONSHIPS 171

- Why Discipline in Marriage 172
- A One-Man Show 174
- Motivation 176
- A Subconscious Desire to Improve...177
- Realizing the Ideal Spouse, May Not be so Ideal 179
- Tackle it All at Once..180
- Acquiring Buy-in From Your Spouse 183
- Is Marriage a Compromise...184
- Time to Accept and Make a List...186
- Roles and Responsibilities 189
- Ego and Humility..190
- What Does Gender Have to Do with it?..192
- Empathy 193
- Conflict Management...195

- What Does a Great Relationship Look Like?......................................196
  - *Twenty Tips on How to Build and Maintain a Great Relationship* *196*
- Conclusion—The Beginning to Your Destiny 200

CHAPTER 9: GOVERN YOUR HEALTH 203

- Managing Your Health Must be a Daily Priority 203
- Exercise Consistently..204
  - *Ten Tips to Help You Exercise Consistently*................................ *204*
  - *Ten Tips to Help You Manage Your Meal Intake*........................ *208*
- Conclusion—Let's Toast—to a Healthier and Happier YOU 212

CHAPTER 10: CONTINUOUSLY STRATEGIZE 215

- Besides, You Will Never Be Satisfied—Enjoy the Feeling 217
- Strategize on How to Minimize or Better Yet Eliminate Those Bad Days..218
- Grade Your Performance DAILY 220
- Conclusion—Status Quo is Failure 223

EPILOGUE 225

- Oh, What a Feeling—Taking Control of Your Life 226
- It's all about that Legacy..228

ABOUT THE AUTHORS 231

- Harris Kern...231
- A'ishah Khan...234

Foreword

Society Says...

All my life I knew one thing, I was a top performer at most everything I did. Until I reached my early thirties and my health took a hit. Everything I had known as a constant in life changed—my career, my friends, my projects, my highly coveted office, my routine, my health, my looks—the many things I had excelled at in life slipped through my fingers like the grains of sand on a beach. The more I grasped, the quicker it all escaped. Pushed into a life of unknowns, I was forced to take on responsibilities and roles I had never wanted nor experienced. Until one day I hit my threshold and an awakening occurred. I realized that although I had excelled at many things in life, the truth was, I had only attempted things I knew I could do well. Whether I truly enjoyed them or not, it was a fail-proof way of living.

Completely frustrated, I turned to the Internet and, as though by divine intervention, came across my soon-to-be coach and friend—Mr. Harris Kern. Working with Mr. Kern I realized the subliminal impact society has had on our way of thinking. Brainwashed by what Mr. Kern often called, "complete and utter NONSENSE," I believed life and I were fragile. After all society says…

- You must sleep at least eight hours a night
- Your happiness is not dependent on finances
- You should never overexert yourself
- Your life is not meant to be difficult
- You should never push yourself if you don't feel well
- You can always find a quick fix for everything
- You will only succeed if you take on what you can handle
- Your weekend is here, it's time for fun and relaxation
- You must finish one goal before moving on to the next
- You shouldn't exercise every day, your body needs a break

These are just some of the false message's society has been pontificating on us for eons, playing a major role in the way we think and operate. Do you honestly believe you will accomplish your goals and achieve self-mastery if you buy-in to this? These self-limiting beliefs ingrained in our minds serve no other purpose than to handicap us. With a little pixie dust magic, we believe that simply "hoping" for the best will magically summon Prince Charming to waltz through the door . . . fixing all of life's problems.

Wake up and smell the coffee! Life is hectic and the demands are endless. We are told to "live life to the fullest," but have we ever really stopped to ponder what this means. Although we may not realize it, living life to the fullest actually requires you to push yourself beyond your limits. Practically speaking, "All men are NOT created equal," in that what is good for one person is not necessarily good for another. To move forward in life, one must begin by learning how their minds and bodies operate. Only then can we use this knowledge to differentiate bad pain from good pain to be able to push ourselves forward. Then, just when we think we've hit our limit, we push a little more. The ultimate goal—do what you love, and the work becomes play.

Having worked with Harris Kern, I now stand in front of the mirror with a better understanding of who I am, including my strengths and weaknesses. Defined by each, I have acquired a new-found strength to push myself to new-found limits. In the process mistakes are inevitable, but as long as you are honest with yourself and others, life will always turn out okay in the end.

—**A'ishah Khan**

Preface

I thank you for selecting this book as a source of guidance. I've poured over four decades of experience into this piece in the hopes of helping you *build the best version of you!* My experience ranges from mentoring over 700 coaching clients to working with almost 150 different Fortune 500 and Global 2000 companies. From parents, soldiers, entrepreneurs, Uber drivers, students, police officers, executives, even a professional prostitute, you name an occupation and I've probably mentored someone from that field. In fact, my experience has reached all six continents, leaving only Antarctica yet to be claimed. Why is this important to you? Because as you read this book, I want you to know that practically any issue out there, regardless of age, sex, nationality, financial status, marital issues, cultural barriers, you name it, I've seen it and dealt with it. Having worked with a variety of clients, my experience is applicable to everyone.

Yet, who am I to tell you my writings are the words of wisdom you should follow? Why should you listen to me? Life is precious and my passion to help individuals be more productive is second to none. Regardless of my experience working with others, more importantly I walk the talk and have practiced what I preach every day of my life. Living life with urgency, adamant to not waste a minute of it, I have been able to: exercise every day of the year, travel all over the world, establish several successful businesses, purchase my first home at the age of nineteen, raise a wonderful family, achieve financial security by the age of thirty-eight, publish over forty books in multiple languages, and even train my mind to only sleep four hours a night. While I am not here to push my hardcore lifestyle on anyone else, unless they so desire, my goal is to help you gain the discipline needed to accomplish *your* goals so *you* can be successful and happy.

In fact, the superseding goal applicable to all aspects of my life is DISCIPLINE—the catalyst for all of my success. However, regardless of how disciplined I became, I also needed to develop my Emotional Quotient (EQ) to manage *my* emotions and to better understand how to maneuver through highly emotional situations—especially when dealing with other professionals. Therefore, to live a fulfilling life you need to be disciplined and possess a high EQ. Whether it's the way I control my emotions, manage my relationships, maintain my motivation, achieve my financial goals, attain spiritual gratification, maintain my health regimen, or even excel in my businesses—discipline and EQ are the key mechanisms through which I train my clients to view and manage their life. After working with me, my clients learn to basically eat, sleep and even shit, discipline. As I have always emphasized, *once discipline becomes the defining element in your life you can achieve almost anything; without it, you struggle to exist.*

In fact, often out of desperation to improve, individuals google the word *discipline* to find me. Having failed achieving lasting change with other life coaches, these persons contact me because they're unproductive (super undisciplined) and squandering their life away. At this point you might be asking yourself, what makes my method different from others? The answer in short is: my technique requires seven days a week accountability. Most life or success coaches facilitate a one-hour a week appointment to help you develop personally and professionally. This is total bunk! To date you've been unproductive your entire life—to break these bad habits will require a continuous commitment on your part and that of someone who will partner with you to hold you accountable to your goals and obligations. The effort involved to become consistently productive by being efficient in every aspect of life is not easy, so please don't ask me how long this transformation will take as no two individuals are alike, but I promise you will see results immediately. My technique is unique as it requires you to be held accountable (initially by me) to your obligations, tasks and goals *seven* days a week, while helping you train your mind so you can eventually hold yourself accountable.

Witnessing my life coaching clients transform their lives, become efficient, and accomplish their goals is a feeling that is indescribable and something I would like to help you achieve as well. Throughout the years, my clients have helped me refine the concepts in this book, although they didn't know this, and I didn't realize it at the time. I have fond memories from all of them. Similarly, I hope you the reader take away from this book the importance of adopting my principles for success and happiness, leaving you with memories that are just as fond.

If you need further assistance on how to strategize to make the most out of your life, I am offering 45 minutes of complimentary consultation via telephone: 818.404.9248, Skype, What'sApp, FaceTime or you can meet with me in person if you live near my homes in Frisco, Texas or Fort Lauderdale, Florida. You can also e-mail me at harris@harriskern.com.

—**Harris Kern**

Introduction

One-third of your life is spent sleeping, one-third is spent working, the remaining one-third *should* be *priceless*, but unfortunately, it's not treated as such. In fact, much of your life is an afterthought, causing you to squander away a minimum of four hours a day due to poor self-management. You're not realizing that to take control of your life it's important to focus on pursuing excellence in *all* areas of life. Your odds of success will greatly improve, as you finally become consistently productive. So, fasten your seatbelt and get ready, you are moments away from unlocking the truth to *Building the Best Version of You.*

Until now, you had little choice but to get up and be at your place of employment on time and perform your duties. The discipline required to enact this ritual daily is instinctual and mostly driven by the fear of not getting paid. However, once the workday ends your mannerisms go by the wayside, you let down your hair and have fun without adhering to any discipline. Unfortunately, this mentality is addictive and almost impossible to turn off and be productive again. Resulting in a miserable struggle, as you attempt to complete your household obligations and goal-related tasks before another workday begins.

Part of the problem lies in our society's view of the word *discipline*. Currently, the word is rarely used at home or in the office. Rather, the most common place you hear the word used is with professional athletes in rigorous training or occasionally at the gym amongst some hardcore bodybuilders. Mentioned elsewhere, it is usually in the context of punitive punishment. Discipline should not be viewed as punishment or couched as something negative. On the contrary, mentoring on the importance of discipline is the best gift a parent can instill in their child.

In fact, the lens through which you view the world must be *discipline* to achieve self-mastery with everything you do. Being disciplined will take you to new heights and the rewards are second-to-none. For example, imagine the feeling of seeing your awesome invention being sold like hotcakes on Amazon. Feel the excitement of seeing your own authored book on the shelves of a bookstore. Imagine having enough money to buy whatever you desire or how about doing something that positively impacts others. Stop and ask yourself, "How badly do you want to see your dreams become a reality?"

In this book, I share with you the *Ten Principles for Success and Happiness* (Chapters 1-10). In my quest to consolidate my years of mentoring into a finite number of beliefs, the number wavered quite a bit. Until one day things fell into place and "ten" became the defining theme. Each chapter is a key principle for *Building the Best Version of You*.

For me, this book fulfills my vision of helping others by designing a strategy for personal and professional development that is simple and easy to follow, a manual of sorts that provides the proof and not just the hype. The *Ten Principles* highlighted in this book are proven, as I have used them to mentor over 700 individuals and 150 organizations, spanning four decades of my life. In fact, I owe my success in life to acquiring discipline along with maturing my EQ. There is no doubt in my mind that the principles highlighted in each chapter are the core drivers you need to make your dreams a reality!

How it Started for Me

Keep in mind, I was not always this way. My story dates back to when I was thirteen years old barely making it through school. My neighbor, Jim Jarman, on the other hand was in his forties and what a specimen he was: intelligent, handsome, great physique, nice home, car and a beautiful family of four. I looked up to him and we often clowned around trading sarcasm most days of the week. Until one warm summer California day, when my neighbor Jim was outside mowing the lawn. It was this day I heard those five magical words that would change my life forever: "Harris, you look like shit."

He was right, and I knew it. At the time, I stood six feet and two inches tall and weighed one hundred thirty-five pounds despite eating everything in sight. I was a weakling who was always bullied in school. I hated life and I hated school. Always the last person picked to play on sports teams, I was called crater face due to my acne. Basically, I was the school outcast. Everyone knew of me, but for the wrong reasons. If I turned sideways, you would not be able to see me. "Harris," Jim said, "eating massive amounts of food is not the way to approach your problem. Your body needs a major overhaul and it doesn't start with your mouth." At thirteen, I did not understand what he was trying to tell me. He continued, "If you decide to follow my instructions to the letter, I will help you out. I want you at my house every Monday, Wednesday, and Friday by four, not a minute late. If you're late, the deal is off—no second chances." Jim was like a drill sergeant instilling in me discipline, starting with the easiest form: punctuality. I agreed, not having a clue what was forthcoming.

Three days a week of torture, always pushing me harder than the one before. What a rude awakening. There was weight training, running, swimming and, most importantly, lecturing. He tested me every day. He would always keep me focused on the exercise and our long-term objective, while teaching me to never rely on anyone else but myself when it comes to acquiring *discipline*. After all, athletes know eighty percent is in the mind, especially on those days you're too tired or stressed out and not in the mood––that's when you push yourself the most. Looking back, I realize what an illusory mind game the entire ordeal was. He was training my mind more than my body, although I did not know it at the time.

Why I Wrote This Book

Once I started developing my self-discipline, my physique and then my confidence naturally followed. The more confident I became the more I accomplished. Jim taught me that I could achieve anything I wanted if I was disciplined. He truly cared and wanted me to be the best I could be. Yes, I had made it! Leaving me with the desire to give back and help as many people as I could make it on their own and always be productive. My experience with my mentor helped me realize my passion in life and allowed me to see what our society was missing.

This book fills a large void in our current day education system, which focuses primarily on didactic learning, leaving a gap in our youth's everyday skills. They are growing up without the structure needed to balance all aspects of life. After my life changing experience with my mentor, I devoted my life to this path of continuous improvement. If a scrawny, academically challenged kid could be independent and successful by the age of nineteen, with his own home in the San Francisco Bay Area, anyone could do it...and this book is here to teach you how!

You Have the Power

Begin by asking yourself the following questions to help determine if this book is right for you. Do you really like what you see in the mirror? Are you happy with your current lifestyle? Would you like your life to be more organized? Do you wish you could be more consistent with your exercise routine? Would you like to have a few extra hours at the end of each week? Do you wish you could be more sincere with your commitments? Would you like to be motivated every day? Do you wish these questions would end? If any of these questions helped you realize there is a void in your life, you should find this book helpful regardless of where you stand today. In fact, this book aims to transform the following bad habits that have become commonplace in our society:

- *Not holding yourself accountable*
  This is where the rubber meets the road. Most of you cannot hold yourself accountable to your daily obligations and the myriad of tasks associated with your goals. The primary method used to hold yourself accountable *every* day is to *train your mind* to be your own cop. Learn how to instill the proper mindset for success.

- *Complacency is your mode of operation*
  Although you have a full plate of obligations and responsibilities, you're unmotivated, but your mind is telling you there's plenty of time. Also, there is no urgency to accomplish your goals and if you miss another goal completion date there's always tomorrow, right? This type of mentality instills complacency. The more complacent you are, the lazier you become. You blink and another five years have passed by again with no significant accomplishments. It is crucial to *train your mind* to live life with urgency and make *every* day count.

- *Not focused*
  You're distracted! Either wasting precious cycles living in the past, dwelling on things out of your control or you're thinking about your friend's drama rather than your goals. Learn how to stay laser-focused on your goals and priorities.

> The issues above among others are addressed in Chapter One

- *Not managing your emotions*
  Managing your emotions and knowing how to respond to highly emotional individuals will be critical for establishing and maintaining good personal and professional relationships. How can you make sound decisions and communicate effectively if you can't manage your emotions? You can't! Learn how to develop your Emotional Quotient (EQ), which most experts believe is more important than your IQ.

- *Not managing negative situations*
  Negativity will derail your progress on any given day. Learn how to manage those "bad hair" days by developing your EQ.

- *Having poor inter-personal skills*
  You have insecurities and lack the confidence to make sound decisions. You also possess poor communication skills. Addressing your insecurities and knowing how to communicate properly will be paramount for success.

> The issues above among others are addressed in Chapter Two

- *Failed goals*
  You set unrealistic goals, you become overwhelmed, you don't manage them, and then voila, another year of failures. Learn how to set and manage your goals to improve your odds for success.

- *Idea's overflow—you lack the discipline to deliver*
  As an entrepreneur your ideas spew out uncontrollably. You believe most of your ideas are brilliant, and I'm sure some of them are, but very few if any come to fruition. You don't establish goals properly and you can't manage yourself effectively. Learn proper goal setting and management techniques, while instituting discipline into your life.

- *Living an unbalanced lifestyle*
  You focus most, if not all of your resources on one or possibly two major areas of your life. Not realizing that in order to live a balanced lifestyle you must learn how to focus (equally) on the Four Priorities of Life: *finances, career, relationships* and *health*.

> The issues above among others are addressed in Chapter Three

- *Procrastination*
  You push things out (i.e., important projects, obligations and tasks) until the last possible moment and occasionally you default because you run out of time or an unexpected emergency arises. Learn how to make every minute count and stop the procrastination for good.

- *Poor time management*
  You waste a minimum of four hours a day on being inefficient and getting distracted. These are common problems with many individuals. When you live life haphazardly, without structure (being disorganized, not following a to-do list and not adhering to a routine) you will continue to waste time. Learn how to manage time by instituting structure and following our seven tips on how to manage yourself to utilize time efficiently.

- *All circuits are busy—Technology overload*
  Not even realizing it, you waste exorbitant amounts of time on the Internet, hours upon hours of "uncontrolled" use: surfing aimlessly, gaming, spewing social media nonsense, texting endlessly. *Building the best version of you* means a completely new way of thinking about yourself. Treat your life as a business and your livelihood depended on its success. Adopting a disciplined lifestyle will allow you to manage technology effectively and stop the wasted cycles.

> The issues above among others are addressed in Chapter Four

- *Wasting time lounging in bed*
  You waste an exorbitant amount of time lying in bed every morning. Snoozing for up to thirty minutes, more on the weekend. You need to have a daily ritual prepared (a to-do list and AM routine), to hit the ground running. That to-do list should include tasks that will advance your major goals. This will make it easier for you to wake up with a purpose—to live life—big-time!

- *Poor quality of sleep*
  This happens for many reasons: talking to a friend late at night, eating junk food before going to bed, engulfed in social media late at night, etc. You need to start managing your sleep (before, during and after). What does it mean to manage your sleep? A key component to improving the quality of your sleep is following an evening routine to wind down properly before going to bed and having a good AM routine to jumpstart your day.

> The issues above among others are addressed in Chapter Five

- *Poor financial management*
  You're in debt, you don't know how much you spend each month, and you have little to no savings. Learn how to consistently manage every aspect of your finances and make it a daily priority.

- *Administrative responsibilities are an afterthought*
  Occasionally you forget to pay a bill, or you lose important documents that may be required for tax preparation. Life's

mundane yet important clerical responsibilities rarely get done, until it becomes a necessity. Learn how to consistently perform administrative responsibilities.

> The issues above among others are addressed in Chapter Six

- *Not managing your job or career effectively*
  Perhaps you work a dull 9-5 job and it's leaving a big void in your life. You feel uninspired to get out of bed each morning. Or perhaps you've been in the same career for a while, but you feel stuck and not sure on how to learn new skills. Unfortunately, you probably do not have a strategy, which would identify a career path with next steps—something that can motivate you daily and help you earn the big bucks.

- *"I never have the time to start a side business—too busy working my day job"*
  At least that's the excuse I hear the most from aspiring entrepreneurs. If you don't live a disciplined lifestyle, you will never have the time to initiate new ventures. Learn how to finally start that side business.

> The issues above among others are addressed in Chapter Seven

- *Opposites with different goals*
  You struggle to improve yourself in every facet of life but feel held back by your partner, who is unmotivated. Many arguments and major conflicts ensue, as you struggle to

find common ground. It's important to have a few shared household goals (i.e., managing to a budget or home improvement projects).

- *Not managing your relationships effectively*
  Proactively managing your relationships (personal and professional) is a priority. Learn how to improve and maintain good relationships with your spouse, colleagues, friends, management, etc.

> The issues above among others are addressed in Chapter Eight

- *Can't exercise consistently*
  You begin exercising again and you go like gangbusters for a few weeks and then your undisciplined mannerisms kick in and it's back to business as usual—using every excuse in the book not to exercise. Follow my ten tips and learn how to exercise consistently.

- *Can't maintain an ideal weight*
  Managing your eating habits is usually an afterthought until your doctor tells you that you're at major risk and/or some health-related issue arises unexpectedly. Putting meal management on the backburner is a *huge* mistake that will catch up with you sooner than later! Utilizing my ten tips for managing your meals will improve your odds for living a long and healthy life.

> The issues above among others are addressed in Chapter Nine

- *Not enough hours in a day to accomplish your goals*
  There will always be more things to do than hours in a day. Typically, family responsibilities, long hours at work and errands gobble up your time with little to no resources available to invest in your goals. You will learn how to continuously strategize to improve your overall performance to accomplish more. Whether it's implementing your morning routine, prioritizing your obligations or organizing your workspace, you can always do better.

> The issue above is addressed in Chapter Ten

Unfortunately, for the undisciplined the above issues are commonplace and are stopping you dead in your tracks. However, the more disciplined you become the better able you will be to counteract these common "bad habits." You have a simple choice; instill discipline or continue to squander your life away. To help you answer the question, ask yourself this: Do you want your kids to end up unproductive like you?

What to Expect—Visualize a New You

Many of my former life-coaching clients, before seeking my services, were looking for quick fixes from articles, books and attending seminars on success. They were looking for something that would get them motivated and give them that slight edge every day. With a ton of material on the Internet to choose from, you can find new content every day for the rest of your life. Unfortunately, these are all short-term highs and nothing more. Stop the nonsense and stop wasting precious resources on short-term solutions.

After years of coaching others on self-improvement, I realized that self-development was not a static process. Rather, it exists on a spectrum ranging from UNPRODUCTIVE at the bottom to SELF-MASTERY at the top. For those of you who are visual, I created the following Maturity Model. It shows us at quick glance where someone currently lies on the spectrum and could serve as a reminder, a kick in the ass if you will, to stay on track. There are five levels; with the pot of gold at the top of this model being the best you can be. Most of my clients come to me either at the UNPRODUCTIVE or ADEQUATE levels. The goal is to develop their life skills and get them to the STRUCTURED level as quickly as possible. Once structured, the journey towards being DISCIPLINED can begin. As you can see it is a stepwise process that involves a slow climb upwards, eventually to the level of SELF-MASTERY. Below is a closer look at the characteristics that define each level.

Maturity Model for Personal and Professional Development

SELF-MASTERY

Wisdom, authoritative, visionary, leader, lives life with urgency, legacy set, excellent communicator, superior EQ skills

DISCIPLINED

Driven, adaptive, manages time effectively, goal oriented, continuously strategizes, resilient to complacency, accountable, manages sleep optimally

STRUCTURED

Routine oriented, organized, adheres to a to-do list, consistent, exercises daily

ADEQUATE

Exists, procrastinates, inefficient

UNPRODUCTIVE

Inconsistent, unreliable, wastes time

The following chapters are the key ingredients—your strategy to help get you to the SELF-MASTERY level of the Maturity Model. However, if you begin reading this book under the assumption that following a small sub-set of steps will produce a new you, you have already set yourself up to fail. What I can guarantee is that with hard work and perseverance, you will see incremental gains over time. Depending on how significantly undisciplined you are, will determine how long it will take. Remember, you are working on undoing your brain's hard-wiring; it took years to make you who you are, it will take time and effort to change you. Also, expect highs and lows. With every step forward, you may slip back a couple of steps, this is normal and expected . . . just keep pushing forward!

Why These Ten Principles

The following *Ten Principles* serve as the culmination of my life's hard work, the *pièce de résistance*, the cornerstone of self-sufficiency. Which is why I envision this book to be used as a manual or handbook, with clear, easy-to-follow and remember instructions on the importance of adopting discipline and maturing your EQ. This book provides the proof and not just the hype, showcasing the impact my values can have on a person's quest to self-mastery.

After being a practitioner of self-improvement and mentoring others to perform at high levels, I truly believe these principles are the catalysts needed to make your dreams come to fruition. With time, your confidence and focus will be impenetrable, you *will* hold yourself accountable to accomplish your goals, live life with a purpose and operate with urgency. Below are my *Ten Principles for Success and Happiness* representing the ten chapters of this book:

1. *Training Your Mind*
2. *Develop Your Emotional Quotient (EQ)*
3. *Attaining Your Goals*
4. *Time Management*

5. *Manage Your Sleep (Before, During and After)*
6. *Focus on Your Finances*
7. *Excel in Your Career and/or Business*
8. *Manage Your Relationships*
9. *Govern Your Health*
10. *Continuously Strategize*

These principles will serve as your roadmap to achieving the change you've been seeking. The effort required is huge, but the rewards are second-to-none. Think of it like building a small business from the ground up, working around the clock to implement your business strategy and ensuring you have every potential obstacle covered. Getting a small business off the ground is a humungous effort. Managing yourself effectively to be successful is also a herculean effort. It's hard but, is anything worthwhile easy? Therefore, it's important to ask yourself, "How badly do I want it?"

Let's Get Ready to Start

Building the Best Version of You begins by having the proper mindset. This mentality starts with an understanding that it will take major change in the way you operate today. My first words of advice if any of this book is going to make a difference, is for you to start with brutal self-honesty. You've been inefficient thus far in life. Stop telling yourself "There, there, it's okay to fail—just keep trying." The more you fail the more you get used to it. Do you honestly believe ignoring your past failures will help you accomplish your future goals? Failure is an ugly word and often we avoid it. However, to bring about change, you will need to take a hard look in the mirror and get ready to face your shortcomings. Face reality and stop making excuses. You must get tough with yourself and look at your existence differently. It's time to take charge of your life and fix these issues permanently. The first chapter of this book begins with training your mind—I will start by having you take a hard look at yourself.

Chapter 1

Training Your Mind

Training your mind is a mentality shift that sets the stage for you to view the world through the lens of discipline. An attitude adjustment in the way you operate teaching you to be brutally self-honest, to operate with efficiency, to push past barriers, and to operate with urgency. This chapter will give you four very important tools to train your mind to think in this way.

Most importantly, you will gain the ammunition you need to fully utilize, and even maximize, every freaking minute of your life. If you were a corporation, which is the way you should be visualizing yourself, wouldn't you need to manage *You, Inc.* 24x7 to be successful? Of course, you would! Envision yourself as a business with your livelihood dependent on you managing yourself around the clock to ensure its success. There are no days off from this new way of thinking. This is a full–time commitment, seven days a week, 365 days a year. It cannot be accomplished with a part–time effort. That is why so many people fail in their attempts to be consistently productive. It must be part of your daily routine, just like putting your clothes on in the morning, or eating a meal.

Once your mind is trained, it stays with you twenty-four hours a day like the blood that flows through your veins. This will alter your personality. Everyone will notice it. They will see the confidence in your face. You will feel like you can accomplish anything and everything, and you will! There will be no limitations. You will gain a mental toughness; like having a professional trainer pushing you through a one-hour work-out twenty-four hours a day. So, get tough with yourself. Get serious and transform yourself into *You, Inc.* and manage yourself around the clock. This isn't about thinking positively and hoping for the best. It's about having a battle brewing internally every day to pursue greatness.

How to Train Your Mind

Now that I've hopefully got your blood boiling and you're striking punches in the air ready to take on the biggest fight of your life, let's get right into the heart of it. The following are what I have found to be the four most effective ways to train your mind:

1. *Assess your past performance—be brutally honest*
   The first step to any self-improvement journey is to take a hard look in the mirror and realize your starting point. Often, we avoid this and many of you will even completely skip this step. However, how can you honestly train your mind to build the best version of you if you don't take the time to understand your strengths *and* weaknesses.

2. *Treating every day equally*
   Being repetitive with key priority actions trains your mind to operate efficiently. Having a good AM and PM routine and a

to-do list targeting the Four Priorities of Life: *finances, career, relationships* and *health*—and doing the same things (i.e., exercising every day, checking your bank accounts and credit card transactions daily, etc.) repeatedly, will eventually train your mind to make it a habit.

3. *Establish phrases—play mind games*
   On days when your mind just wants to take a break, crawl into bed, and not do anything, repeating hard-core negative phrases or positive affirmations gives you that extra kick in the butt to get you over the hump. These phrases repeated frequently over an extended period, train your mind to push past barriers that otherwise would stop you dead in your tracks and cause you to come up with excuses.

4. *Set an expiration date and live life with urgency*
   If you know when your END date is, you will operate with urgency every day to try and complete your remaining goals. Set an expiration date and train your mind to believe your life will cease to exist on that date. Then repeat that expiration date continuously and you will live like you are dying.

These methods lay the groundwork for the journey ahead, so take some time and fully encapsulate these into your brain's hardwiring. Although it may seem Jedi-like and a bit unnatural in the beginning, what you will soon realize is—it is quite simple! While each method accomplishes a different goal, all of them work to bring you closer to the ultimate goal of "Training Your Mind" to view life through the lens of discipline. Let's get started!

Assess Your Past Performance...Be Brutally Honest

It's difficult to remember the myriad of issues plaguing your progress when they're not front and center. In fact, most people don't take the time to sit down and face their weaknesses. Seems simple enough, but without this key step you are preventing yourself from becoming successful. Therefore, I cannot emphasize how important it is for you to start by seeing where you currently stand and the areas you desperately need to fix. A word of caution: Don't be shocked when you see the harsh reality up close and personal, as your weaknesses will likely far outweigh your strengths.

To begin with, create a table with two columns and answer the questions below. One column should be labeled *Strengths* and the other column should be labeled *Weaknesses*. For the purposes of this book and you the reader, I have formatted these questions to provide simple yes and no answers with key descriptive words underlined. If you answer a question with a <u>yes</u>, then document the underlined descriptive words under the *strength* column and if you answer with a <u>no</u> then document under the *weakness* column. Don't forget, the purpose of the final table is to provide you with a snapshot of where you stand today.

I. *Training Your Mind*

    a. Is your mind trained to consistently <u>motivate</u> yourself to get things done every day of the year?

    b. Do you operate with <u>urgency</u> on a daily basis, as though you are running out of time?

    c. Do you concentrate on <u>one task</u> at a time or do you multi-task?

    d. Do you hold yourself <u>accountable</u>?

II. Emotional Quotient (EQ)

a. Do you respond to <u>emotional setbacks</u> or other major distractions quickly and refocus on your priorities?
b. Do you have good <u>communication</u> skills to help you excel in your career and with your personal relationships?
c. Are you <u>insecure</u>?
d. Do you know how to manage your <u>emotions</u> to prevent conflicts and remain productive?
e. Do you seek <u>positive</u> opportunities when you're in a negative situation?

III. Priorities and Goal Management

a. Do you live a <u>balanced</u> lifestyle, where you spend an equal amount of time on your health, career, finances and relationships?
b. Are you <u>goal-oriented</u>?
c. Are <u>tasks</u> associated with your goals documented on your to-do list?
d. Do you <u>set goals</u> on New Year's Eve, your birthday or some other occasion?
e. Do you <u>manage goals</u> effectively?
f. Do you plan your goals thoroughly and establish <u>milestones</u> with due dates?
g. Do you set <u>realistic goals</u>?

IV. Time Management

a. Do you <u>procrastinate</u>?
b. Do you indiscriminately <u>over-commit</u> (say yes to everyone), causing you to feel overwhelmed and short on time to complete your goals?

c. Do you spend too much time on family-related <u>drama</u>?
d. Do you spend too much time helping your <u>friends</u> and putting your goals on the backburner?
e. Do you <u>dwell</u> on the past, wasting significant time on things you cannot change?
f. Do you waste too much time in <u>traffic</u>?
g. Do you randomly surf the <u>Internet</u> for hours at a time?
h. Do you spend too much time on <u>social media</u>?
i. Do you spend too much time <u>gaming</u>?
j. Do you watch too much <u>TV</u>?
k. Do you spend an exorbitant amount of time <u>texting</u>?
l. Do you maintain a <u>structured</u> lifestyle?

   i. Do you create a <u>to-do list</u> the night before? So, when you get up each morning you have a script of your day's activities ready to go?
   ii. Are you <u>organized</u>? In your home, office, email, car, administrative responsibilities?
   iii. Do you follow an efficient AM and PM <u>routine</u> to make the best use of your time?
   iv. Are you <u>punctual</u> for appointments or are you always 5-10 minutes late?
   v. Do you maintain your <u>administrative</u> responsibilities i.e., pay your bills on time, file paperwork, etc.?

V. *Sleep Management*

a. Do you manage <u>sleep</u> optimally?
b. Do you follow a disciplined <u>routine</u> in the evening to sleep at a reasonable hour?

c. Do you wake up with a <u>purpose</u> *every* day?
d. Do you <u>snooze</u> in the morning after your alarm sounds off?

VI. Financial Management

a. Do you manage your <u>money</u> effectively?
b. Are you <u>financially secure</u>?
c. Do you have a <u>savings account</u> for emergencies or major purchases?
d. Do you maintain a <u>budget</u>?
e. Do you always know your numbers (expenditures, investments, monthly re-occurring bills)?
f. Are you in (bad) <u>debt</u> i.e., credit cards, student loans, high interest rate loans?
g. Do you live from <u>paycheck to paycheck</u>?
h. Do you invest for <u>retirement</u>?

VII. Career Management

a. Do you have a fulfilling and <u>challenging career</u>?
b. Do you enjoy your <u>work</u>?
c. Have you set <u>career goals</u> (i.e., where do you see your career in one year, three years or five years from now)?
d. Do you want to start your own <u>business</u>?
e. Do you have a <u>business strategy</u>?

VIII. Relationship Management

a. Do you manage <u>personal relationships</u> effectively?
b. Do you manage <u>professional relationships</u> effectively?

c. Are your <u>relationships fulfilling</u>?
   d. Are <u>roles and responsibilities</u> clearly defined in your household to avoid friction?
   e. Is your relationship a true <u>partnership</u> where you have joint goals not just individual goals?
   f. Is your spouse or partner <u>lazy and unmotivated</u> and you're energetic and goal-oriented or vise-versa and its causing turmoil in the relationship?
   g. Do you maintain your <u>spiritual obligations</u>?

IX. Health Management

   a. Do you live a <u>healthy</u> lifestyle?
   b. Do you <u>exercise</u> consistently?
   c. Are you <u>energetic</u>?
   d. Do you manage your <u>eating</u> habits effectively?

X. Planning

   a. Are you continuously <u>strategizing</u> to improve your financial outlook, career situation, personal and professional relationships and your health?

These questions were not arbitrarily selected, rather they are derived from hundreds of life coaching engagements that I have facilitated. The following is an example portraying the Strengths and Weaknesses of one of my coaching clients; it's truly an eye-opening experience. It's not a one for one correlation. In other words, there won't be an answer for each question because it may not be applicable.

Strengths	Weaknesses
Communication	Motivate
Positive	Urgency
Family oriented	One task
Learning	Accountable
	Emotional Setbacks
	Balanced
	Goal oriented
	Time Management (Procrastinates, over-commits, social media, gaming)
	Over-commits
	Structured (to-do list, routine, disorganized)
	Snooze (up-to 30 min each morning-more on weekends)
	Financial management
	Career goals
	Health (exercise consistently and junk food)
	Strategizing

The table above allows you to know exactly where you stand the day you start and which areas you need to address. Although it is likely not a pretty picture, keep in mind that you have the power to build these characteristics and combat the issues that hamper your success and happiness. You have the power to make what you want out of your life. Make your life challenging and excitement will naturally follow. If you refuse to accept anything but the best, you'll always get the best. You have no idea how much power your mind possesses and once trained properly you can take on anything.

Treating Every Day Equally

Treat every day equally (be repetitive) and it becomes habitual.

How many of us carry out key daily actions without thinking; like walking, speaking, or even driving a car? This automatic ability to do something with little or no thought is often referred to as being on "autopilot" or what psychologists call automaticity. As defined by Psychology Wiki, "automaticity is the ability to do things without occupying the mind with the lower-level details required, allowing it to become an automatic response, pattern, or habit." Doing the same things repeatedly, will eventually train your mind to make it a habit.

In various areas of our daily lives, we often create habits to tackle more complex tasks. This makes tasks simpler by freeing up our attentional resources, so we don't become overwhelmed. We can function quickly and efficiently without giving attention to every little detail. Imagine how difficult life would be if you had to think about each step you take while walking! When training your mind, I am asking you to use the positive aspects of automaticity to focus on the priorities of the day.

With that said, *treating every day equally* means just that—being *repetitive*—with key "priority" actions to train your mind to operate so *efficiently* the actions become *habit*. It means fulfilling your most important obligations—your priorities—*every* day of the week. When your priorities become habit, you gain a sense of efficiency and flow that maximizes your use of time. Now I'm not suggesting for you to become some workaholic, rather I am emphasizing the need to focus on your priorities *first* every day. Attacking them early, *every* single day of the week, ensures a sense of accomplishment and satisfaction that carries you through the day as you tackle the more menial chores of life.

This discussion would not be complete without mentioning the *Four Priorities of Life*, which will be covered in more detail in Chapter Three. For now, simply know that to have a balanced and fulfilling day you need to target each priority, in some form or other, every day. The task actions within each priority are different for each person based on his/her life goals. For example, one of my current clients prioritizes as follows: Health includes cardio exercise, career includes her job responsibilities as a pharmacist, finances include checking her accounts daily, and relationships includes morning spiritual readings with God. Although the amount of time devoted to each task within the priority varies based on that days' work schedule, repeating the same tasks first every single day eventually makes them habitual.

You may be wondering, "How can every day be treated the same? What about weekends, holidays, or even vacation?" I agree, it would be ludicrous to put forth the same effort seven days a week—after all, everyone needs a break to recharge. Not to mention, we all have days when life's menial chore lists take precedence due to their sheer length or time sensitivity. For days like these, modify your list as needed. For instance, you can do a lesser amount of each priority task or take on a subset of it. The following are a few common examples:

- *Weekend—day off*
  What if you don't want to do anything on a Sunday but relax and watch TV? It's simple—just plan ahead and put a bit more effort into your priorities throughout the week or on Saturday. Then you can feel totally free to goof off and relax when you decide to, without feeling guilty.

- *Holiday—day off*
  For days when you didn't put the forethought into planning ahead, do a subset of your priority actions. If you normally read a chapter from your spiritual book each morning, modify and read ten minutes instead. That way you will still get your priority actions done, but early enough in the day to still enjoy your holiday day off; after all, these only come around a few times a year.

- *Vacation*
  Now you may think it's crazy to focus on your priorities even while on vacation. On the contrary, it's easier to continue to *treat every day equally* than be stressed out on your first day back. Who wants to return to work and see a thousand emails in their inbox? Spending even ten minutes at the start of the day cleaning out the clutter will keep you organized when you return from vacation. Or if you exercise every day, you know how great you feel afterwards—why would you stop? Rather than the full one hour in the gym, you could do at least twenty minutes of cardio or better yet, incorporate exercise into your vacation activities—i.e., if you're into nature, go for a hike or a swim at the beach—and make it a part of your vacation.

Essentially, by *treating every day equally* you are directing your energy and training your mind to focus on your priorities so that you are productive every single day. It is so easy to get overwhelmed by all the nonsense distractions of life, being pushed around by these outside forces, you never accomplish your goals and end up feeling very dissatisfied. You are the captain of your ship, so take control. The payoff will be that you accomplish your goals.

I can hear the internal flack now: "That's utterly ridiculous, there's more to life than just thinking about your priorities" or, "Does that mean I have to work all the time?" or, "I can think about what I want to think about!" or, "I am tired and hurting why should I continue to torture my body." These are all protests from your mind fighting the control. Your mind is used to having no control, sort of like a spoiled child. So of course, it is going to give you a hard time and try to throw you off. Fight your mind when it goes down this path of thinking. It is your life, so you should control the direction in which it goes—take control of your mind and energy.

Establish Phrases—Play Mind Games

On days when your mind just wants to take a break, crawl into bed, and not do anything, repeating phrases—hard-core negative or positive—gives you that extra kick in the butt to get you over the hump. These phrases train your mind to push past barriers that otherwise stop you dead in your tracks and cause you to come up with excuses. When negative situations rear their ugly head, know the phrases you want to use and start repeating them over and over and over again, until your mind takes over and pushes you forward. It might seem strange at first, talking to yourself, repeating phrases you are not accustomed to hearing, but with time it will help retrain your mind. The key is to not waste time and move yourself forward quickly.

Playing this type of "Mind Game" can be done with one of two types of phrases: negative phrases or positive affirmations. After years of working with a variety of clients, one thing I have learned is that the only way to know which type works for you is through trial and error. I would prefer if I could tell you positive phrases worked better for a certain gender or personality type, but that has not been the case. So, go ahead, pick one type, positive or negative, and give it a test run for about a week. You'll know if the phrase is working for you based on whether you are able to redirect your mind and get moving without wasting time. There is no right or wrong with this, so be patient as you work to figure out which phrases hit your hot button!

For me personally, the phrases I use to redirect myself and stay focused are hard-core negative ones. Think about it, a drill sergeant barks out orders at a recruit and the recruit listens and executes ASAP. The sergeant's voice is loud and whatever phrase is used hits the mark immediately—nothing is sugarcoated. For me, these phrases resonate within and get my attention faster than others. I find the negative phrases practically cancel out the negative emotion I am feeling, leaving me with positivity.

On the other hand, positive affirmations can work wonders to retrain our negative, and often self-sabotaging, thinking patterns. Like how we exercise to maintain and improve our physical well-being, positive affirmations are exercises for the mind. With time and repetition, the goal is to reprogram our thinking patterns toward a more positive outlook. In fact, studies have shown positive affirmations improve problem-solving abilities of those impacted by stress, help treat persons with low self-esteem, depression, and other mental health conditions, and even stimulate areas of our brains responsible for positive healthy behaviors. *If you're struggling with negative thinking, write down your bothersome thoughts then rewrite them as their opposite positive version. Ensure it is realistic, written in the present tense, and don't forget to say it with feeling!*

REFERENCE:
https://www.mindtools.com/pages/article/affirmations.htm

So, let's get started and discover which phrases will wake you up, perhaps get you upset, and ultimately motivate you to finally do something to improve your life once and for all? Playing mind games by repeating phrases must be taken seriously to train your mind to combat your weaknesses. The following are a few examples of phrases you can use to "Play Mind Games" that cover the top three areas that most individuals have difficulty with; exercising consistently, completing goals and getting out of bed promptly.

Phrases and Tips to Help You Exercise Consistently

It's easy to get bored with your exercise routine and lose motivation. Likely, the first solution that rears its ugly head is: "I need a break." Wrong! Never assume taking a *break* will solve the problem. Below are some phrases and tips you may consider using to help you train your mind to maintain consistency.

Repeat the following positive affirmations:

- Each day I exercise, the healthier I feel and the more energetic I become.
- I know it's hard to exercise, but just imagine what fun it will be to show off a size six dress at my reunion. (Visualize yourself in that dress and how you'll feel when you're getting those looks of admiration).

Repeat the following negative phrases:

- I wear clothes that hide my fat—how long do I want to keep doing this?
- If I take today off, I'll want to take tomorrow off—this cycle will NEVER stop—JUST DO IT.

- I'm a wuss—do I want to be one for the rest of my life?
- Push yourself—you loser!
- Every day I take a break is another day wasted.

Phrases and Tips to Help You Prevent Goal Failure

How many times have you told yourself this line, "I missed my goal's due date—it's no big deal—I'll just push the date out a few more months—I have too much going on right now." It's the same old pattern on repeat.

Tell yourself repeatedly:

- If I fail just one goal, I will fail all my goals. I'm tired of failure. I don't want to continue this pattern for the rest of my life.
- Failure is unacceptable.
- I am running out of time to accomplish my goals. Next month I will be XX years old, and I keep pushing goal due dates further out—this pattern will continue until the day I die. I need to change now.
- When I die a picture will be placed on top of my casket and that will be the end of me. At the end of the ceremony—the only thing left will be that picture. Leaving behind a legacy is just a pipe dream and will never become a reality unless I make it happen.

Phrases and Tips to Help You Get Out of Bed Promptly

Most of you have the most difficult time getting out of bed. You will use all types of tricks to convince yourself to stay in bed for just a few more minutes. Your internal saboteur will throw everything at you to derail your progress and keep you in that bed longer.

Tell yourself repeatedly:

- Another 10-20 minutes lounging around in bed every day adds up to hundreds of hours of wasted time for the year. Extrapolate that wasted time and shock your system!
- If I'm exhausted, another ten minutes of sleep will not help. *It will not!*
- Remember that to-do list I created last night and all those obligations that *must* get done today?
- If I keep hitting that snooze button today, I will do the same thing tomorrow and the next day. It will never end, so stop the pattern today!

Repeating phrases to train your mind may sound a bit weird, but it's the best way to keep yourself on top of your goals. You need to determine which phrases leave their mark, cause you to redirect yourself quickly, and help you stay focused on your priorities. Remember, your objective is to get on with your life as quickly as possible, not to wallow in depression. The nastier the situation, the more challenging it will be to train your mind to stay on track toward a more productive life, but I know you can do it.

Set an Expiration Date and Live Life with Urgency

I dare you to ask yourself, "How badly do I want to accomplish all of my dreams and aspirations before I DIE?" Life is precious and time flies by ever so quickly. You blink and another year has passed with nothing to show for it. Making it crucial to live *every* day to the fullest. Most of you already realize the need to stop wasting time, but this is easier to pontificate than to practice daily. The thought of death is scary, but it is necessary to acquire the urgency needed to accomplish all your goals.

One of the most effective ways to train your mind to consistently live with urgency is to set an expiration date on your life, just like any carton of milk. If you know when your *end* date is, you will operate with urgency to try and complete your goals. Set an expiration date and train your mind to believe your life will cease to exist on that date. Then repeat that expiration date continuously and you can "live like you are dying". Trust me, I know from experience, it works like a charm!

Although I wish I could take credit for this ingenious idea, I was taught this by my mentor Jim Jarman back in my early twenties. I asked him how I can consistently accomplish more in a shorter amount of time. He said, "Believe you are going to die soon and that you actually know when you are going to die." I looked at him like he had two heads, but I never questioned him. Based on his advice and my goals, I selected the age of forty as my expiration date. I kept telling myself (training my mind) several times a day—to hurry up and accomplish my major goals before I die at the age of forty. I had seen too many people give up on their dreams and live with regrets, and I didn't want to be such a statistic. I wanted to leave behind a legacy for my future kids, so I pushed *hard* and accomplished the following major goals. I actually beat my goal, and by the age of thirty-eight I was able to:

- Save at least one million dollars
- Acquire over one million dollars in assets

- Own three homes
- Pay cash for a luxury car
- Become Vice President of a major corporation
- Travel the world
- Publish a book
- Own one of the nation's top muscle cars and speed boats, which actually graced the cover of Hot Rod Magazine in July of 1975
- Never miss a day of exercise
- Become a muscular person: I went from being a 6'2" 135lb weakling to a 6'2" 200lb man of muscle
- Strengthen my relationship with God: never missed a day of nightly prayer, completed a year of studies to convert to Christianity, and lived by the Ten Commandments

Living with a sense of urgency allows you to draw upon greater resources. Think for a moment about the saying, "necessity is the mother of invention." How true this statement is! In fact, it is the necessity to accomplish your goals by a certain expiration date that gets your mind working. When things are too comfortable, you tend to coast along forgetting that time is passing you by and your goals are being left undone. You get distracted. You complain about nonsense, such as your food not being cooked right. Or you obsess over whether you made the right decisions or not, although it's too late to change anything. Rather, once your mind is properly trained to believe your time on earth is limited, you gain a sense of urgency and productivity naturally follows.

Conclusion—Straight from Yoda's Mouth

Your mind is the best tool and greatest asset you have to build the best version of you. Use it wisely and regularly to help you get ahead. Your mind will rarely need a break, so take advantage of it. The sooner you harness its strength to work in your favor the better. You train a muscle to perform a desired movement or motion, similarly you train your mind to obtain a desired concentration, attitude, drive, and motivation.

In Chapter One: *Training Your Mind*, I established as one of the tools in your armamentarium to achieve *discipline*, remember the sky is the limit! Once your mind is trained to be that guiding force behind all your actions then and *only* then will you be successful. Your mind will be set to autopilot and it will constantly nudge you forward, even when you're tired and feeling lazy. The execution is automatic as your mind takes over and adheres to your priorities. If you try to disengage from *autopilot* forget it—your mind won't let you. Your mind is now controlling your body *every* day. It is the guiding force.

With that said, our mind is comprised of not only our logical/reasoning side but also our emotional/intuitive side. To live in harmony, it takes a balance between these two opposing forces. Often a person is swayed more heavily on one side or the other, Discipline is achieved when we correct this imbalance. Training your mind is ascribed to Chapter One for a reason: It's by far the most important *Principle* and the most challenging, but the rewards are second-to-none.

The next chapter dives into the topic of improving the Emotional side of your mind to achieve the ultimate goal of building the best version of you.

—Harris Kern

Chapter 2

Develop Your Emotional Quotient (EQ)

"There is a world of greatness inside of you. Your emotions are the key."
—*Unknown*

If discipline is the door to opportunity and growth in your life, then emotions are the key without which the door of discipline is inaccessible. Not being able to manage your emotions will derail your progress forward every step of the way. How can you make sound decisions if you don't manage your emotions? You can't! We all have bad hair days, that is normal, but what matters is how you manage your emotions to overcome these negative situations. Then, once you can manage your emotions you are better prepared to interact with others. For the fight against an external source is easier; it is the fight against our own internal self that is the greater battle.

Our fast-paced technologically driven lives have become so "independent" we forget that our society's success is contingent upon each person being able to work with others within society. In other words, you must learn to get along with others . . . *Introverts* included. Working with Mr. Kern, he shared with me the following perfect case study example: In a nutshell he was an isolated introvert, thirty-five years of age. After a year of coaching, this is what he said to Mr. Kern, "I knew I was an introvert, and I used to pride myself on this. I looked at life black and white. Lying, cheating, killing and stealing are wrong; if I lived by the values of honesty and fairness, I believed I was set for life. I said things the way I saw them, no need to sugar coat it. As long as I was honest, and my intentions were good, others would comply, right? Oh, how wrong I was! Somehow, I truly managed to seclude myself from reality until the age of thirty-five, when all hell broke loose. Each day was a shocking truth; and the emotions that I kept buried so deep began to take hold of me." This client had no clue the importance Emotional Quotient (EQ), or lack thereof, played in his life!

EQ Defined

The definition of EQ, or what is commonly referred to as Emotional Intelligence (EI), according to Wikipedia is: *The capacity of individuals to recognize their own, and other people's emotions, to discriminate between different feelings and label them appropriately, and to use emotional information to guide thinking and behavior.* Although you may be hearing this term for the first time, EI actually dates to a paper published in 1990, followed by a book written by psychologist and *New York Times* reporter Daniel Goleman.

To simplify the term, your EQ is basically comprised of your inter-personal skills or how well you get along with others. This includes the ability to manage your emotions and to communicate effectively so you can build relationships. Take this a step further and it also includes the ability to identify and understand other people's emotional gestures, so you can react in an appropriate manner. In fact, many people believe EQ has a greater impact on your life than your IQ ever will. Making a high EQ coupled with discipline a powerful combination.

In fact, based on more than 700 life coaching engagements by Mr. Kern, individuals with a high EQ are the happiest, communicate the most effectively and get the most done. Think about it for a moment: If you are super productive, operate with urgency, confident in your abilities, possess the gift of gab and know how to nurture relationships you *will* be highly successful. In fact, most professionals agree that IQ accounts for only 10-20% of the ingredients needed for success. While being disciplined and having a high EQ comprises the remaining 80-90%!

Take this a step further and it's important to realize that EQ is not limited to relationships at the workplace, but rather includes your ability to empathize and negotiate with individuals in your personal life as well. As the saying goes, if you can tackle the emotions at home, you are prepared to handle the world outside of it. Take this a step further and you see that a high EQ also includes being able to recognize your own emotions, and their triggers, so you can articulate them in such a way that is respectful of the emotions of others. We are looking at a tri-level hierarchy when it comes to EQ, working from the inside out: first understand yourself (self-management), then use these skills to work with those closest to you (relationship management), and then work on your inter-personal skills in society (social management). Gaining an understanding of these categories is the first step to being able to develop these skills.

The Three Categories of EQ

The following are the three categories of EQ in order of importance:

1. *Self-Management*
   Being in "control" of your emotions. You have very little control over when a disruptive emotion (i.e., depression, anxiety or anger) occurs, but what you can control is how long it lasts before it does some real damage. Someone who manages their emotions effectively would have the following attributes:
   a. Adapts to changing situations
   b. Controls disruptive urges
   c. Re-directs emotions to avoid conflict
   d. Learns to forgive his/her self
   e. Is responsible for his/her own performance
   f. Maintains morals: respectful, honest, kind, not pre-judging, keeps commitments, has integrity
   g. Possesses an even-keel demeanor at all times: doesn't get too upset or too happy
   h. Self-confidence in his/her capabilities and self-worth
   i. Makes sound decisions *not* based on emotions

2. *Personal Relationship Management*
   Developing and nurturing personal relationships. Being in tune with your own emotions (self-management) enables you to understand the emotions of others so you can effec-

tively manage relationships with those closest to you. Someone who manages personal relationships effectively would have the following attributes:

a. Recognizes emotions in others and understands their feelings
b. Possesses awareness of the impact his/her emotions has on others, especially in spontaneous, tumultuous or sensitive situations
c. Articulates appropriate messages
d. Brokers deals when communicating sensitive issues with others
e. Knows how to negotiate with people who have a high IQ, but poor EQ skills
f. Adopts new ideas with flexibility

3. *Professional Relationship Management*
Developing superior interpersonal skills is crucial to succeed in your worldly life. I refer to it as *people smarts*. This is vastly different from *personal* relationship management as your life outside the home often includes strangers, people whose personal stories you are not privy to, and maintaining the fine line between work and personal life (it is business after all, feelings aside, the priority is getting the work done). Someone with strong professional relationship management skills would have the following attributes:

a. Manages conflicts: does not take sides, deals with the facts to settle disagreements
b. Negotiates fair settlements between multiple parties
c. Portrays leadership to guide and inspire others

    d. Is an agent of change: has the ability to introduce and manage change effectively
    e. Collaborates with a multitude of personalities to deliver shared outcomes
    f. Influence's others in the appropriate direction

The above three categories are a simplistic way of looking at something quite complicated, as there is quite a bit of overlap between the three areas. Although complicated to understand, the promising news is: EQ is a skill that can be acquired and improved with practice. This begins with the realization of the importance of having a high EQ in all three areas of your life. EQ effects not only how we manage our own emotions but also how we deal with the emotions of others and this is especially important when attempting to have serious discussions involving sensitive issues.

How to Improve Your EQ

Emotions are one of life's paradoxes. Emotions give you feedback and tell you things: what you're afraid of, when somebody is violating a boundary, or what makes you happy. Emotions, such as fear, anger, grief and hopelessness have their place and serve a valuable purpose. However, it's getting stuck in these emotions that causes problems. Keep in mind, as emotions go high thinking goes down, making the balance between the two ever so important.

With a better understanding of what EQ is and the aspects of your life affected, the remainder of this chapter highlights ways to improve your EQ skills. Based on Mr. Kern's experience working with a variety of clients ranging in EQ proficiency levels, these are proven approaches to a calmer and more balanced mind-set. These techniques target all three categories of EQ, from your self-management to your personal and professional relationship management. Master these and you will be ahead of the game, but always remember it will take time and patience as you attempt to undo years of mental programming. Working on your EQ is not an easy task, but with courage, motivation, and an openness to learn how others perceive you to be, you will see change.

Learning to Forgive Yourself

On the path to managing life effectively, Mr. Kern explains one of the biggest struggles he has seen with clients, especially the over-achieving perfectionist types, is their ability to forgive themselves. Until you learn to love yourself, you cannot expect to fully give to others. Recall one of the key instructions given prior to a flight taking off, "before helping others with their oxygen mask you *must* secure your own mask first." We often give and give of ourselves until we are depleted of not only energy and focus, but also love and self-compassion. As mentioned earlier in the book, the path towards building the best version of you requires patience as you face many setbacks. Therefore, being able to forgive yourself with love will be pivotal in helping you push forward.

As an example, the following is a case study of one of Mr. Kern's clients. This young woman was raised in a family, where being the only responsible member she was pushed into the role of matriarch while constantly being questioned and critiqued on her every action. Her internal dialogue quickly learned to emphasize, on a repeated basis, how pathetic she was for *each* and *every* mistake, no matter how big or small. All mistakes were looked at equally; what a fallacy! Research shows that the way we speak to ourselves, our internal dialogue, is the way our parents spoke to us growing up. Then as we mature, inevitably the way we speak to others reflects the way we speak to ourselves—our internal dialogue. Therefore, please be kind, gentle, yet firm and fair with your internal voice and the way you speak to others will naturally follow.

In fact, being kind to yourself will help propel you forward in all aspects of your life. Rather than beating yourself up for a mistake, with self-compassion you are transforming the mistake into a positive by learning from it. For instance, one way you can practice replacing negativity with self-compassion is as follows: Rather than saying, "I am so dumb, how could I have let this happen?" Change this to, "I am moving forward. I had a lapse in judgement, but I forgive myself." I would practice this technique first before moving on in the chapter. Once you can forgive yourself more, you will be better equipped to practice the other lessons.

Keep Your Cool—Manage Your Emotions

After learning to be more forgiving of yourself, the next most important EQ skill is the ability to deal with any negative situation without letting your emotions get in the way. How do you learn to do this? First, realize it will take practice. This means you must face the issues that evoke these negative emotions head on, no more avoiding such situations. When you run away from conflict and unpleasant emotions you have relinquished power and control, without which discipline will be difficult to attain. Secondly, remind yourself that facing your fears is evidence of your immense courage. Even the mere fact that you are reading this book shows you have courage! Use this newfound courage to face your negative emotions and continually practice, with time it will become easier and easier, guaranteed.

Thirteen Tips on How to Develop Your EQ

When emotional impulses do arise, the following are some of the easiest and most practical ways to defuse your emotions and develop your EQ muscle immediately:

1. *Stay focused*
   Stay focused on the present; face what is being said and what is being done without wondering about the past. How do you apply this daily? By focusing your mind on your to-do list which includes obligations in your personal and professional realm, you are left with very little time for anger or worry about something or someone else. Each time an incident arises that can derail your emotions, remind yourself of that to-do list and the need to stay on track to avoid wasting time.

2. *Meditate*
   When you notice your emotions are taking over, become aware of your breathing. Focus on your breath as it enters and exits the body at a focal point (i.e., nasal passage or stomach), then when your mind does wander gently bring it back to your breath. Start with as little time as you like and slowly increase the amount of time in focus. Meditation, like lifting weights to build muscle, helps build the mental strength you need to stay focused.

3. *Go for a walk and be mindful of your surroundings*
   If possible, taking a walk or break in nature is a great way to relax the mind. Try to really focus on the natural details of your environment.

4. *Become aware of your body*
   Utilize body scans, a mindfulness tool that helps you listen to your body and notice physical sensations to obtain insight into how you are feeling. For instance, tension in your shoulders or jaws while driving to a friend's house may be a sign that this relationship needs attention.

5. *Feeling down—turn on the lights*
   Research has shown light is directly linked to mood and learning. So, if need be, turn on a brighter light in your area or open the shades and let the sunshine in.

6. *Expect that life will present you with challenges—avoid being surprised*
   Life is meant to spike up and down, similar to a cardiac EKG monitor. When the lines move up and down you are alive. If life were a straight path this would be shown on an EKG monitor as a flat line, which correlates with death.

7. *Mr. Kern's favorite—exercise*
   Getting blood pumping through your body and especially to your brain is not only good for your health but also your focus.

8. *Try journaling your feelings and thoughts daily*
   Purging thoughts from your mind onto paper gives you the mental clarity you need to focus on your priorities. In addi-

tion to journaling your feelings, the following three journal ideas help you anticipate difficult situations, stay positive and track your growth:

a. Describe a situation that would be difficult for you and think of various ways you could respond to it—goofy, silly, mean or super nice. The idea is to have several options for responding to a variety of difficult situations.
b. Morning gratitude list—jot down three quick items you are thankful for. This type of journal helps redirect your mind to keep you focused on the positives in your life.
c. Daily Good Decision Log—think back through your day and log at least three good decisions you made that you are proud of. This type of journal provides positive reinforcement and highlights the changes you are making.

9. *Read fiction books*

    There is evidence to support that reading fiction books can help increase your ability to empathize. A 2016 review titled *Fiction: Simulation of Social Worlds,* explores the idea that fiction allows us to transport ourselves into the lives of other people, invariably helping us better understand others, which in turn we can use to improve our ability to interact with them. https://www.cell.com/trends/cognitive-sciences/fulltext/S1364-6613(16)30070-5

10. *Identify your emotional triggers*

    Think of a time you lost control of your emotions and deconstruct the incident to pinpoint the instigating factor. You could even keep a log of these times to help you identify your emotional triggers, or weak spots. Identifying these triggers will help you learn to react more appropriately the next time you come across one, which believe me will happen.

11. *Know your strengths and weaknesses*
When you are self-aware of both your strengths and weaknesses, you will have realistic expectations of yourself. This will allow you to know when to turn to others for assistance, saving you a lot of time and potential heartache.

12. *Pause and take a deep breath before acting*
Rather than allow your emotions to take the wheel, take a moment to visualize what your ideal self would do instead.

13. *Understand your feelings*
Oftentimes when we lash out at people, we are actually venting frustrations from earlier in the day or even the week. Take the time to understand the root cause of your emotional outburst and remind yourself that all emotions are temporary. This too shall pass.

Possess an Even-Keel Demeanor—Plan for the Worst

"If you say that someone or something is on an **even keel**, *you mean that they are working or progressing smoothly and steadily, without any sudden changes."*
—*COBUILD Advanced English Dictionary*

Applied to daily life, this translates to avoiding the highs and lows of your emotions while taking everything in life with stride. In other words, don't get too excited during the good times and learn to control your negative emotions during the bad times. It is especially important to be prepared for the bad times as life is comprised of setbacks—guaranteed—there is no avoiding it. I'm not saying always expect doom and gloom, but rather, always remember it's not *if* bad times will arise, it's knowing how to manage your emotions *when* they arise. With this in mind, how will you keep your cool when the next surprise comes your way? This 2,000-year-old Taoist proverb is a good starting place to help you answer this question:

> *There was a farmer whose horse ran away. That evening the neighbors gathered to commiserate with him on his bad luck. He said, "May be." The next day the horse returned but brought with it six wild horses and the neighbors came exclaiming at his good fortune. He said, "May be." Then, the following day his son tried to saddle and ride one of the wild horses, was thrown off, and broke his leg.*
>
> *Again, the neighbors came to offer their sympathy for the misfortune. He said, "May be." The day after that conscription officers came to the village to seize young men for the army, but because of the broken leg the farmer's son was rejected. When the neighbors came in to say how fortunately everything had turned out, he said, "May be."*
>
> Short Story: The Taoist Farmer
By Sofo Archon

The moral of this story is that no event alone can truly be judged as good or bad, lucky or unlucky, fortunate or unfortunate, as only time will reveal the entire truth. Therefore, it is a waste of time to invest a ton of emotional energy into daily events, whether good or bad, as we don't really know the final consequence. Rather, maintaining an even-keel demeanor is a sign of wisdom that brings comfort in accepting what comes your way and making the best of your circumstances. Remember the saying, "When life throws you lemons, make lemonade!"

However, being able to control your emotions, to not over-react nor under-react, as with everything else in life requires practice! Start by always remembering to *plan for the worst while hoping for the best.* By planning for the worst, you are mentally prepared for life's daily setbacks so that you are not taken off guard. The main reason people *react* emotionally is because they are surprised by these setbacks. Although we cannot anticipate what the setback will be, anticipating its definite arrival allows us to control our response by eliminating the surprise component. In fact, the more you practice managing your response to life's daily minor setbacks, the easier it will be to cope with the bigger tragedies of life that are inevitable (i.e., loss of employment, breakups, medical emergencies, and deaths).

Always remember, controlling emotions is crucial to remaining productive. When faced with a setback, stop yourself and think about what's important in your life. Don't sit there and stew in the negativity. Managing your emotional reactivity to life's daily setbacks will save you precious time, energy, and focus—limited resources, which should be handled with care. In fact, how you deal with life's setbacks says more about your character than how you deal with success. When the *shit hits the fan,* and I promise you it will, do you want to be remembered as the person who lost their temper or the person who calmly turned to the right people for advice and came up with solutions? Uncontrolled emotions can be disastrous depending on how foolishly you let your emotions take control. Ultimately, the decision on how you react is yours.

Redirecting Negative Emotions

In addition to *planning for the worst while hoping for the best*, you can also turn to the "Establish Phrases—Play Mind Games" technique discussed in Chapter One: *Training Your Mind* to redirect negative emotions. This technique is very useful when dealing with emotional conflict, whether with yourself or with others. If you recall, it requires you to frequently repeat either negative phrases or positive affirmations to give you the extra kick in the butt you need to get you over the emotional hump. Mr. Kern taught me to use these mental phrases to move the negativity aside and push myself forward to focus solely on my daily to-do list and goals. The more hardcore these phrases are, the less time you spend thinking about the negativity and the more time you spend being positive and living life with urgency.

Whether you utilize negative phrases or positive affirmations is person dependent and will take trial and error before you learn which works best for you. The following are a few examples of both. Whichever one you choose, always remember to say each with passion and conviction.

Example One
An experience related by Mr. Kern: "I had a very difficult breakup in my late twenties—I was distressed. It was someone whom I loved very much. I lost focus, energy and motivation, but within twenty-four hours I was back to normal due to a few phrases I said to myself repeatedly: "*She's a loser,* she's going to regret leaving you; I'm

better off without her; She's probably with some other guy right now; She's not worth it..." Did I really feel that way? No way! However, I trained my mind to believe she was not good for me! These key phrases made me angry enough to transform the negative emotion into *powerful positive energy* and got me back on track quickly. The objective was to not look back and dwell on the past. The past was over, and I needed to put things behind me and focus on the future. Life must go on—the sooner the better."

Example Two
Let's say you get into a big fight with someone close to you—you're in a bad mood and you don't feel like doing anything. You may want to try these phrases to snap you out of it.

- Precious minutes are being wasted—you're a fool to let this stupid fight drag on.
- The argument is over—stop dwelling on it—it gets you nowhere.
- You can't win—who cares who wins—it's irrelevant—give in—you have more important things to do.
- She/he is a wonderful person—don't be stupid.

Example Three
A client of Mr. Kern was about to be promoted into a management position for the first time in his career. On one hand he was excited, but on the flipside, he knew he would have to occasionally speak in front of an audience. Whether it was in front of his colleagues or people from other departments, this client was afraid to death of public speaking. Based on research, Mr. Kern trained his client to

spend at least a few minutes reminding himself about his best qualities, especially before any event that increased his anxiety or stress. In particular, the following affirmations boosted his confidence:

- I *can* do this!
- I know the content well and have rehearsed my presentation dozens of times.
- I am well-respected throughout the company as a top performer.
- My boss and colleagues *will* like my presentation.
- The content of my presentation is unique and of interest to everyone in the organization.
- I am positive every day and the day of the presentation will be no different.
- I will do it with enthusiasm.

REFERENCE:
https://www.mindtools.com/pages/article/affirmations.htm

Working with Difficult People

One of the biggest obstacles you'll face as you're "building the best version of you," is keeping your cool when dealing with difficult people. It is extremely difficult to hold yourself accountable when dealing with these persons, as it involves more than just your own emotions and actions. Think about it, you are now dealing with another human being whom you have no control over. Difficult people when unmanaged can be one of the biggest time wasters of all!

We've all been in these situations, when someone ruffles your feathers for one reason or another. The first step in this situation is identifying which group these difficult people fall into: Value-added or Value-deprived. Below are some tips and examples on how to better manage these two groups of people. In the beginning, as you are learning to decipher which group a person falls into, when confused err on the side of caution and assume they are value-added. With time, the delineation will become clearer.

Value-added individuals

Are you required to deal with this person to move on to the next step in your life, whether personal or business? If the answer is yes, they are a *value-added* individual. Recognizing this allows you to remind yourself that although they are difficult, they still add value to your life. This helps you take a deep breath and muster the strength needed to push forward, knowing it is for a better cause. In addition to positive redirection, here are a few tips to help you deal with these unavoidable yet value-added *difficult* people:

1. *We do what we must*
   If it's your boss, you have no choice but to remain calm, listen and *obey*. Mr. Kern refers to it as kissing butt. Even if you know he/she is wrong, you have no choice but to comply to keep your job!

   In your personal life, although things are not as clear-cut, once again remain calm, listen and *never be confrontational*. For example, Mr. Kern had a client who was quite particular with her hair. She had gone through multiple stylists until she found one that both colored and cut her hair to her standards. However, every so often the stylist would miss a spot of color and would get quite defensive when asked about it. Seeing that this stylist was a Value-added individual, Mr. Kern's client had to learn how to maneuver the situation to not rub the stylist the wrong way yet get the job done to her satisfaction. A great example of how to do this is to always start with a compliment, share the blame if needed, and ask nicely. For example, "I really loved the way the color came out last time, could we start with the front of the hair again? I think I wash my hair too often and the color seems to bleed out of the front the fastest." Always remember, no one is perfect. Since the stylist did a great job, it was worth the extra time it took to figure out a way to work around the stylist's defensiveness. As Mr. Kern would say, "It's just another form of kissing butt."

2. *Be apologetic*

   Simply saying sorry or that you will do everything in your power to fix the situation can go a long way in defusing many negative encounters.

3. *Give people the benefit of the doubt*

   Any one of us could have a bad hair day. This doesn't mean that we're all jerks. *You have no idea what the other person is going through in his/her life.* So, don't label someone in a derogatory manner based on an isolated incident or two. Rather, give everyone the benefit of the doubt. Stop and investigate your assumptions before making a judgement on the other person. Ask yourself, "could something else be going on?" and try not to assume the worst-case scenario. Having positive thoughts results in positive emotions and ultimately positive behaviors…and who doesn't want that!

4. *Don't put up with too much of their emotional outbursts either*
At a certain point, you must draw the line and maintain your self-respect and emotional sanctity. You have the right to be assertive and state the following in a calm relaxed manner, "Please do not speak to me in this way."

5. *Be flexible*
No two people are alike. This is a fact. There isn't one script that fits all situations, and you can't look at the world through one (very narrow) lens and treat everyone equally. Being flexible is especially a key success factor when communicating with highly emotional or rigid individuals who cause friction. *Your responses will need to differ for every difficult person.*

Value-deprived individuals

Is this person irrelevant to your goals—but just happens to be in your pathway? If the answer is yes, they are a *value-deprived* individual and should be avoided. Not only is this person a waste of precious time, but he/she is also detrimental to your health and well-being. Remember, you have more important things to do with your time. Be respectful and resourceful in finding ways to bypass them. In this situation, I highly recommend "white lies." If you are not hurting another person or cheating them out of their due rights, a small excuse to save time is often the only way to gracefully manage these individuals. Below are a couple of examples to help you deal with these value-deprived *difficult* people:

Example One (impromptu discussions)

How many times do you walk the hallways at work, and someone stops you to chit chat? If you added up the minutes wasted by these impromptu meetings, it would be truly eye-opening. If these discussions do not pertain to your job function, then you have little choice but to politely cut them off. For example, "Excuse me Ted, I would love to speak with you right now, but I have an urgent matter I must address back at my desk. Please let's catch up next week." Of course, by next week something else will come up—Ted will eventually get the hint. It's as simple as that!

Example Two (meeting scheduled, but change in plans)

Out of peer pressure you set a lunch date with an acquaintance, only to realize later that family obligations have unexpectedly increased leaving you with little time to spare. Considering this person is a value-deprived individual (you weren't really that enthusiastic about this encounter in the first place) and family-relationship goals are a priority, make up a little white lie (i.e., I need to take my daughter to soccer practice). If truly needed, re-schedule the lunch date for another time. For now, your time is too valuable!

Conflict Management—Influencing Others in the Right Direction

Conflicts happen continuously; between family members, with personal relationships, in society between different organizations and is quite common with professionals at the office. According to www.businessdictionary.com the definition of conflict management is: *The practice of recognizing and dealing with disputes in a rational, balanced and effective way. Conflict management implemented within a business environment usually involves effective communication, problem resolving abilities and good negotiating skills to restore the focus to the company's overall goals.* I would also include your personal life (i.e., joint goals with your spouse). Conflicts are intriguing and infuriating. Below are my nine tips on how to influence people in the right direction.

Nine Tips on How to Influence People

1. *Find common ground*
   Try and find common-ground topics that are not political and always start with positive information. This helps any conversation begin to develop and is important to help create a bond with the person. Bonding with someone is especially important prior to dealing with negative issues. Once the conversation is flowing and a level of comfort is established, it is easier to interject the conversation with something negative, making the negative news easier to swallow. If this doesn't work and a diplomatic solution cannot be reached, ask to reconvene at a different time and/or venue. Do not force or demand a conclusion.

2. *Think outside of the box*
   What does this mean? As issues arise think strategically and provide solutions—don't just complain about things. Not being judgmental, and rather being empathetic, allows you to keep the emotions low so you can think in this manner.

3. *Never raise your voice*

   Arguing doesn't help anyone—avoid it at all costs. In many instances, when you're trying to have a healthy discussion and you're dealing with sensitive issues, often it turns into a heated conversation. Do not raise your voice or yell. Raising your voice doesn't serve any purpose except to make a highly emotional issue worse.

4. *Envision the big picture*

   Always envision the big picture/overall objective. What do you want to get out of this discussion? Keep the endgame in sight and don't go down to their level of negativity. Quickly adapt and change the direction of the conversation: Remember sh** happens frequently and comes at you from all directions, especially when dealing with people who have poor EQ. If you can't manage their emotions, then adjust your overall objective keeping the endgame in mind. Unfortunately, there are those combative types who enjoy being argumentative. You need to avoid the temptation to argue. When you encounter these types, remember to start the conversation by finding common ground as explained earlier. If you do get into an argument, never try to win, instead find a cordial solution. Always try and converse versus argue.

5. *Hide your arrogance*

   From a young age we are trained to hide our insecurities. When focusing on developing your EQ, it is also very important to hide your arrogance. This ability will help you influence others in the right direction. So, the next time there is a disagreement, swallow your pride and check your ego at the door. Even if you feel you are right, pick and choose your battles and focus on ways to recognize others.

6. *Always be diplomatic*
   With any conversation, you can't always have it your way. It's a two-way street, not a one-way highway. Within the issue at hand, look for commonalities that the two of you agree on. If there are some, build on them as this will make the difficult aspects of the issue easier to tackle. Remember, it requires give and take to reach an understanding. Be diplomatic, negotiate and never demand anything.

7. *Ignore irrelevant comments*
   Occasionally, people will say the most upsetting things during conversations. I've had that happen to me on many occasions, but I let the negative comments come in one ear and quickly exit the other without hesitation or further thought. Remember your end goal and focus on it to help you ignore the flagrant comments made by others to purposefully derail the conversation. Only you will lose.

8. *Improve your empathy skills*
   Reading the emotions of others, or empathy, is a key element in improving your EQ skills. It will help you choose your words wisely and influence a conversation in the right direction. For example, if a conversation is going down the wrong path and you're not sure what the other person is feeling, just *ask*. Never be afraid to directly ask what the other person is feeling. On the flipside, also remember to empathize without getting too emotionally invested. The reason being, when

emotions go up thinking goes down and you lose sight of the end goal. As with everything else in life, it's a balancing act.

9. *Put yourself in their shoes*
   Momentarily stop thinking about yourself and try to see things from the other person's perspective. Determine what's important to them and if possible, try and understand their strengths and weaknesses. The more you know about someone, the easier it will be to influence others and conjure up the appropriate message to achieve the best results. Additionally, treat others the way they would want to be treated, not the way you would like to be treated. If they feel like you truly understand them, it will go a long way in helping you achieve the overall objective.

It's How You Communicate

Communication is key. If you have the gift of gab, it will help you excel in every facet of your life. We are social creatures, inter-dependent on each other to thrive. Unfortunately, our technologically driven lives afford us the ability to live increasingly more independent than just a decade ago. However, at one point or another you will need to work with others if you want to excel in life and achieve more. Mr. Kern explains, he has had clients who have attempted to live life independent of others, learning the hard way that one aspect or another of their life suffers drastically. To avoid the turmoil caused by poor communication skills, and to get things done in life, you *must* learn how to communicate with others. The good thing is, this too is a learned skill requiring practice. As Albert Mehrabian explains (*https://www.toolshero.com/communication-*

skills/communication-model-mehrabian/), successful communication is made up of three parts: the words you use, your tone of voice and your body language. Practice the following fourteen tips and you are on the path to acquiring successful communication skills.

Fourteen Tips on How to Communicate Effectively

1. *Be honest*
   Speaking truthful is always the best policy.

2. *Be respectful*
   Respect individuals and their space. Treat others as you would expect someone to treat you and don't try to force your opinion down their throat. Also, don't criticize or judge their point of view.

3. *Listen—don't do all the talking*
   Effectively communicating means listening to the other person intently. When you listen to someone it shows that you respect their discussion points. It may not work out to a 50/50 mix, but a 60/40 mix will go a long way to having a successful outcome. Never do all the talking. If it's all one-sided you may not get the outcome you desire.

4. *Be real*
   If you portray phony mannerisms your counterpart will turn the discussion off in a heartbeat. Individuals who display an authentic demeanor will be effective communicators.

5. *Be mindful of your voice*
   It's not just *what* you say, but also *how* you say it that matters. The sound of your voice can change the perceived meaning

of a message. Ensuring your voice matches the meaning of the message is important. For instance, relaying negative information with a cheerful voice can be rude and offensive. At the same time, being mindful of your voice is important to help prevent underlying messages from coming through that should be kept private. For instance, if you are assigned to tell someone they are being promoted but personally feel they are bad for the job, you will need to be mindful of your voice to ensure your annoyance is not conveyed. A person's voice is made of the following components: articulation, pronunciation, tone, pitch, and projection. Each of these components requires practice for success. The following are a few quick ways to improve your voice:

a. *Speak clearly*
Don't mumble or speak too quickly—articulate and pronounce your words carefully to ensure your counterpart can understand your message.

b. *Don't be monotone*
Use the pitch, volume, projection and even inflection of your voice to emphasize words as needed and keep a listener engaged. The size of the room, the number of people being spoken to, and even the length of your message are some factors to consider when determining how to use these aspects appropriately.

c. *Always pay attention to the tone of your voice*
Don't come off as unapproachable. Be passionate, upbeat and enthusiastic when appropriate.

6. *Watch your body language*

    Practice in front of a mirror and watch your facial expressions, body stance, eye contact, and posture. Keep in mind culturally appropriate maintenance of space and touch as well. Along with *what* you say and *how* you say it, what you *don't say* can be even more important. In fact, research shows 55% of communication is made of non-verbal cues and is important as it conveys what a person is *feeling*. For example, a person yawning is often interpreted as boredom.

7. *Be aware of your emotions—stay neutral*

    Don't let your emotions obstruct your message as negative emotions will create barriers. If you seem down, impatient, have emotional outbursts or promote negativity you will always lose your audience. You know when you're having a good day, a so/so day or a bad day. Therefore, before initiating an important conversation make sure to leave any negativity at home. Think of the positives in your life to help re-direct your focus. If this isn't possible, then it's best to re-schedule the encounter. If rescheduling isn't an option and being positive is coming off as fake, get through the encounter by maintaining a neutral demeanor. A neutral demeanor means not getting too excited or displaying negativity in your voice. Neutrality along with being mindful of your voice and body language will help you get your message across appropriately.

8. *Do not beat around the bush*

    For general conversations get to the point quickly without ever being rude. It's important not to waste anyone's time. For highly sensitive and especially unfavorable conversations you may need to sugar-coat your words a bit. However, being sensitive to the others person's feelings does not require you to be long-winded; you can still deliver the message in a timely fashion.

9. *Be polite*
Say please and thank you throughout your conversation at appropriate times.

10. *Be complimentary*
Giving compliments works wonders as many individuals don't recognize their strengths. When deserved, being nice and giving praise are very important to have a meaningful discussion.

11. *Don't pry and don't get too personal*
Self-explanatory.

12. *Facilitate private discussions in person (if applicable)*
Never email or text important discussions. If possible, discuss highly sensitive issues in person even if this delays the conversation. It's important to view someone's facial expressions to be able to adjust the conversation as needed. If meeting in person is out of the question, say you live in a different city, then a phone call is the next best thing.

13. *Know your audience*
Who is the person or audience you will be speaking to? Learning important "general" cultural, religious, or even local information before the meeting will help you better prepare. For example, knowing the city's favorite sports teams or popular food items will help you better engage your audi-

ence. While learning about their culture will help you avoid behaviors that may be discouraged. If acquiring this information before the encounter is not possible, try to arrive early and speak to the early arrivers or even open the conversation with some general questions: "What do you do for a living? What are your goals and hobbies?" Be genuine when asking these types of questions and be sincerely interested in their answers. Although no two people are alike, look for unities between you and him/her. If there are some commonalities build on them.

14. *Electronic communications*
In addition to the other tips listed in this chapter, always respond to text messages and emails. One of Mr. Kern's biggest pet peeves is when people do not respond. Give the other person the respect of a response, practicing cordiality and accuracy. They took the time to email you, what makes you too important to respond!

An EQ Case Study: The Doctor and His Two Sons

The following is a case study as related to me by Mr. Kern. The names of the family members are fictitious for privacy.

Dr. Robert Davis contacted Mr. Kern regarding his sons: David and Dusty. In their initial discussion Mr. Kern asked Robert what prompted him to contact a life coach. Robert explained: "My boys are good kids, but the eldest son just flunked his first year of college due to a gaming addiction. While my second son, although he is a genius, is not motivated as a junior in high school. Both boys are very intelligent, but without discipline they're both going nowhere."

The good news was both boys knew they had a problem and were very receptive to being mentored. However, the difficult part of this engagement was interacting with their father. Every weekend Robert and Mr. Kern would have a status update via a conference call. Days prior Mr. Kern would tense up. Just the thought of speaking to Robert would eat Mr. Kern alive. Despite having been warned by Robert's wife and two sons about this, no one had ever said anything to Robert. Although Robert's IQ was extremely high, his EQ was lower than anything Mr. Kern had witnessed before. It was hard to understand how such a highly respected physician, earning more than half a million dollars a year, was clueless when it came to interacting with others. After several months Mr. Kern couldn't take it anymore, and he finally sent Robert the following email titled, *Robert and EQ*.

> *Robert, as you know the health and success of the Davis household is my utmost priority. Therefore, whenever I can interject some wisdom in a respectful manner, I feel compelled to do so. Please forgive me in advance if I am crossing the boundaries of my responsibilities, I just care big time! If you recall a few months ago we identified the strengths and weaknesses of each person in the household. I've added the following additional issues to your personal list, which are all related to EQ:*

- *Ineffective communicator*
    - *Rigid (drill sergeant) mannerisms*
    - *Not diplomatic*

- No compassion whatsoever
- Inadequate email/text communication practices

- *Not flexible when trying to manage others*
    - *It's perceived to be your way or the highway*
    - *Treats everyone equally (expectations are one-sided)*
    - *Only sees the world through one (very narrow) lens

- *Emotional outbursts during brainstorming sessions and status update conference calls*

- *Inability to adjust expectations*
    - *Fighting battles that don't need to be fought*
    - *Not envisioning the big picture/overall objective*

But Robert...Who am I to highlight these issues? After all you're highly successful—right? This is a fact. Being successful in your career is a huge accomplishment, but to consistently win all the battles life throws at you, you also need to manage your relationships. I believe you are completely unaware of your EQ shortcomings and therefore implore you to please take my advice seriously. You truly are a caring human being, with a wonderful family. Please heed the following recommendations:

- *Record some of your conversations—listen to your tone*
    - *Be more charming and sensitive when speaking*
    - *Display some feeling*
    - *Do not treat your children like they are your employees*

- *Think several times before speaking*

  - *If you are unsure whether your comments will have a negative impact or offend someone, just remain quiet*
  - *Don't force your methods—swallow your pride*
  - *Be humble*

- *Listen to your wife, make decisions together*

  - *We all have our strengths and weaknesses. Your wife's EQ is her strength. Why not turn to her for her viewpoint before making decisions? She will balance you out nicely.*

Please put your EQ before your IQ in life's pecking order. Your IQ is there—sure you will always keep learning. However, your EQ is much more challenging and more rewarding too. EQ begins with you and branches out to the others in your life. It requires understanding, self-control, responsibility, and optimism. Some of its rewards are the increased ability to influence, communicate with, and inspire others. EQ is based on your attitude towards others and yourself, ultimately building your character.

After sending this note, Robert contacted Mr. Kern a few days later and asked for Mr. Kern's help. They recorded their conversations and over time Robert's tone improved. Robert improved in many of the positive attributes he was sorely lacking. Also, once Robert's EQ improved so did his relationship with his sons, his wife and even his co-workers too! Always remember, EQ affects all aspects of your life.

Transfer Your Emotions and Free Your Mind

Please remember to not overwhelm yourself. As with all self-improvement efforts, it will take time and patience. After reading this chapter, select one area you struggle with the most and focus on improving in that area first rather than tackling multiple areas at once. Stop and ask yourself, "what one area of improvement would give me the greatest benefit at this time?"

After you have selected one area to begin with, turn to others to obtain unbiased information on how you can improve. Seek out those who will be honest with you while still having your best interest at heart. It's important to not turn to those who share your general viewpoint on life as this will provide the same information you are accustomed to hearing. By opening yourself up to a different perspective, you will grow more and learn to interact with a variety of people. Remember, the goal is to broaden your horizons and learn to be adaptable. At the same time, also select a close friend or family member, someone who knows you very well, to be your mirror. This can be very helpful when you are frustrated and unclear on what you are feeling. They can act as a mirror to reflect your emotions back to you, a key asset when faced with emotional roadblocks that are inevitable when striving to change.

Finally, once you've selected one area for change, have obtained feedback from others, and have identified a person to be your mirror, don't waste time…dive in head first! As the old saying goes, practice makes perfect. You must expose yourself to uncomfortable areas to invite the change needed.

Conclusion—EQ is MUCH More Important Than Your IQ

EQ is not rocket science—but it takes effort and time to master, yet paramount to effectively manage your emotions with personal and professional relationships. It's also crucial to read other people's emotions and react appropriately. We need to better comprehend, sympathize and traverse with others or success will elude us in our lives and careers.

Unfortunately, half the people Mr. Kern interacts with don't even know what EQ is and for most people, emotional intelligence is far more important than one's intelligence (IQ) in attaining success and happiness. Developing your EQ skills will take time and will require much practice. With that said, now let's get out of your head and start putting your dreams and aspirations on paper!

Once your mind is trained (Chapter One) and your emotions controlled (Chapter Two) you're ready to move on to Chapter Three. In the next chapter, we jump right in to learning how to not only set your goals, but more importantly how to manage them. In the next chapter Mr. Kern also reveals one of life's biggest lessons: it's important to have goals, but what's more important is prioritizing and balancing these goals amongst what he calls "Life's Four Priorities." Once this is accomplished, the rest just rolls right off your tongue and is a piece of cake, and who doesn't like cake? I do!

—A'ishah Khan

Chapter 3

Attaining Your Goals

Another New Year's resolution—really—putting your hopes and aspirations on a new year?

We all look forward to a new and hopefully better year, but things don't magically change with the stroke of midnight on New Year's Eve. Just because the day on the calendar changes from December 31st to January 1st, does not mean there is going to be a new *You*. Although a person may start the first few weeks of the new year like a gangbuster, their undisciplined mannerisms eventually rear their ugly head putting any progress to a screeching halt. With a foundation relying solely on hope and temporary operational adjustments, it's no surprise New Year's resolutions are one of the biggest deterrents to personal development. Please don't read this the wrong way. Hope is very important, but if you don't fix yourself first then a new day on the calendar will *never* help you accomplish your goals.

Consistently achieving your goals takes a humungous effort! Most self-help publications highlight goal setting and its relevance.

I wholeheartedly agree, however, goal-setting is only one part of the equation for successful goal attainment. There are three key areas:

1. *The Four Priorities of Life*
   I categorize life into four main areas: *Finances, Career, Relationships and Health.* These are life's four most important priorities. If focus is properly maintained in these areas, you will achieve your most significant goals. To attain self-mastery and to live a happy and successful life means excelling in *all* four areas.

2. *Goal setting and goal management*
   The headliner for this chapter is *goals*, which I separate into two sub-sections: goal setting and goal management. There is a *huge* difference between goal setting and goal management. Goal setting includes: careful planning and establishing realistic short-term (minor) and long-term (major) goals. Whereas, goal management refers to the most important activities you need to perform on a daily basis to accomplish your goals.

3. *Maintaining balance*
   When you maintain balance, your goals are focused on excelling equally in all Four Priorities of Life. This can be very challenging as it's easy to focus on one of the four areas while letting others slide—eventually causing some real hardship in your life. However, maintaining balance amongst your goals (in all four areas), inherently means living a fulfilling life. Who wouldn't want a life that is financially secure, filled with career excitement, based on fulfilling relationships, and powered by a healthy lifestyle?

In this chapter, I elaborate on the above three key areas of goal attainment as we continue through the *Ten Principles for Success and Happiness* to *"Building the Best Version of You."*

The Four Priorities of Life

Commonly we hear the world refer to living our lives with a focus on *mind, body and soul.* I completely agree with this categorization. However, *Building the Best Version of You*, there is a bit more to life than just mind, body and soul. Let's be real! You can't live life without money and to have money you must have a career or business. Therefore, I look at life's all-encompassing categories a little differently. My categorical scheme includes mind, body and soul, with a lot more added to truly ensure you can make your dreams of success, strength and happiness a reality. To "Build the Best Version of You", I categorize life into four priorities. When establishing goals ensure that these four areas are front and center in your planning effort. Let's take a closer look at these priorities to understand what each truly includes.

1. *Finances*

   - Budgeting
   - Savings
   - Expense management
   - Investments
   - Multiple sources of income
   - Debt

Poor financial management practices have ruined individuals and many relationships. It saddens me to say, and it's unfortunate, but this world revolves around money. The sooner you make it a priority and manage it effectively, the better you will sleep at night.

2. *Career/Business*

- Climbing the ladder
- Maneuvering through the political landscape
- Managing perception
- Performing at a superior level
- Owning your own business
- Juggling a full-time job with a side business
- Continuous education to develop your knowledgebase

Since you spend so much time working, why not get the biggest bang for the buck and excel in your professional world.

3. *Relationships*

- Spiritual
- Family
- Spouse
- Colleagues
- Friends
- Partnerships

It's easy to lose sight of your family and your spiritual obligations, while focusing on more exciting areas like money, power, immorality and material possessions. Don't go there!

4. *Health*

    - Exercising daily
    - Weight management
    - Eliminating bad habits (smoking, drinking, etc.)
    - Having an endless supply of positive energy (mental and physical)

To be ultra-productive you need to be in good mental and physical condition. Managing your health seven days a week is a must, not only for energy, strength and well-being but also because it helps individuals who suffer from high anxiety or depression. Very few things are as impactful as the rush one attains after a great workout!

There are many ups and downs in life. If you're not proactively focusing on the above areas equally, you are destined for an emergency crash landing with little to no chance of survival. So, before you go down such a path of self-destruction, listen to someone who has been there. Stop ignoring the four most important areas of your life before it's too late for redemption!

Goal Setting and Goal Management

Just about everyone sets goals, but how many people actually accomplish their goals? Unfortunately, this is an easy question to answer; very few! There are two main reasons for this: Most people do not set goals properly and then completely fail to manage their goals on a daily basis. Setting goals without careful planning and proper management is a complete waste of time. Doing it right is not easy, but getting it right is life altering. Below are ten tips on how to set goals and manage them to fruition.

Ten Tips for Setting Goals

The hierarchy for successful goal "setting" starts with a focus on the Four Priorities of Life, then setting meaningful and realistic goals, and finally mapping out the milestones pivotal to ensuring successful completion. The ten tips below cover this process in more detail.

1. *Keeping life's four priorities front and center*
   When setting goals ensure the Four Priorities of Life are rooted in your planning effort. The goals you set should span across all four areas evenly, so you live a well-balanced life. Focusing on any one area and ignoring others will create imbalance. These priorities encapsulate life and all of them are equally important.

2. *Laying the groundwork*
   Over the years you've likely documented to-do lists, journal ideas, goals and dreams in various locations: on your computer, in journals, on scraps of paper, or even on your phone, to name a few. Consolidate all of these into one "master" list and save on a single file in your computer. Delete any items that are now obsolete and prioritize the ones that are still relevant. Make sure you categorize them under the Four Priorities of Life discussed earlier.

3. *Set goals judiciously—plan thoroughly*

   Most people do not take the time to think through their goals thoroughly. Don't just set goals arbitrarily without assessing your strengths, weaknesses and current lifestyle. Also, every goal needs to be planned thoroughly based on the following criteria:

   a. How long will it take to accomplish?
   b. What will I have to sacrifice?
   c. What other areas of my life will this impact?
   d. Do I have a realistic chance of accomplishing this goal?
   e. Do I have the bandwidth?
   f. What other obstacles could prevent me from accomplishing this goal?

   Your answers will determine whether or not you should proceed in establishing that particular goal. There are no right or wrong answers. Everyone's lifestyle and characteristics are different.

4. *Plan for worst case scenarios*

   Unfortunately, emergencies happen without advance warning. Incorporating the appropriate safeguards when setting goals will help improve your chances of accomplishing your goal on time regardless of any unforeseen emergency. Consider factoring in some cushion time for the following emergencies when setting your goals:

   a. Someone in your family *will* have severe issues to deal with
   b. You and your significant other *will* have a major fall out
   c. You *will* have legal issues

d. You *will* have major financial issues

e. You *will* be laid off from work

It's not if—it's when! You know some if not all of the above issues *will* occur in your lifetime—so be prepared and buffer in extra time for these emergencies. Plan ahead and assume they will occur! If these issues never happen, you're that much further ahead to achieving your goals. Planning for worst case scenarios is crucial for goal success!

A catastrophe is only one if it has never been planned for. Don't let yourself be surprised and thrown off guard. A word of caution: *Continue to be aggressive and remain focused on accomplishing your goals as quickly as possible.*

5. Don't depend on others

You should never set goals that depend on someone else to help you accomplish them unless it's for guidance or an occasional helping hand. Please do not take this the wrong way: you still need experts (contractors, professionals, etc.), you will also need colleagues, friends and family occasionally, but you shouldn't depend on these people to accomplish your goals. For example, let's say one of your goals is to build your own home. You will need specialists along the way and perhaps occasionally a helping hand from a friend. However, don't rely on that friend to always be there to help you accomplish that goal, after all they have their own life challenges and obligations. That responsibility falls squarely on your shoulders. Placing dependencies on others could increase your odds of failure as you cannot control or manage the actions of others. You must own the goal. Sure, it is a lot of weight to carry on your shoulders, but if something goes wrong, there is no one else to blame.

6. *Set minor (short-term) and major (long-term) goals*
What is the difference between minor and major goals? That is for you to decide. Everyone is different. You have to consider the complexity, the magnitude and your current lifestyle before deciding which goals are minor and which ones are major. Some of my minor goals could be considered major to someone else.

Typically, minor goals are: (1) short-term—can be attained in less time than a major goal (they take days, weeks or a few months to complete), (2) simple (a few easy steps), and (3) require few resources. Of these goals, those that take a few months to complete could also be considered a major goal, however, they are branded as minor goals because they are not as impactful as major goals. Below are a few examples of *minor* goals associated with the Four Priorities of Life:

- Finances
    - Open a savings account and automatically transfer a set amount each pay period
    - Establish and maintain a simple budget
    - Monitor your expenses daily

- Career
    - Organize your workspace
    - Never be late to work
    - Review work-related emails three times a day

- Relationships
    - Go on a date night every other week with your significant other
    - Go to a house of worship every week
- Health
    - Lose ten pounds in one month
    - Hire a trainer

Major goals are typically long-term (require over six months and up to several years to complete), require more resources, and will have life-altering effects. You may forget a few short-term/minor goals, but you will *never* forget a major goal! Major goals are always a priority. Also, minor goals can occasionally be cast aside in order to focus on a major goal, which is usually time dependent. Below are a few examples of *major* goals associated with the Four Priorities of Life:

- Finances
    - Purchase a home
    - Have a million dollars in total assets
- Career
    - Get promoted in two years
    - Attain the largest bonus possible every year
- Relationships
    - Get married
    - Start a family

- - Nurture a minimum of one relationship per month with key colleagues and management

- Health
  - Exercise daily
  - Lose 50 pounds

Major goals, if accomplished will help you master your life and solidify your legacy.

7. *Goals should be realistic (in scope and due date—initially)*
   At this stage of your development, the more you take on the greater the chances you will fail. Set realistic minor goals that have attainable due dates and concentrate on doing whatever it takes to complete those goals. It's critical to get accustomed to success with a few quick wins before taking on too much. Possessing a mindset based on accomplishments is crucial for continuous motivation. Once you've instituted structure and developed your self-discipline skills, you can gradually take on more.

8. *Keep goals simple*
   Your life is already complicated and busy with obligations. When establishing goals keep them simple, straightforward and easy to remember. In other words, minimal milestones and administrative overhead. Do not complicate life further with cumbersome and outlandish goals. Avoid complicated goals that take years to accomplish, have numerous milestones, and require you to depend on others along the way. People fail because they set goals that are outlandish and impossible to accomplish.

9. *Never set goals on impulse*

   Many individuals set goals on impulse or momentous occasions. Establish goals regardless of a symbolic date on the calendar. Every goal should be extremely important and thought through carefully with time and resource considerations at the forefront, not the momentous occasion. Contemplate on what you *care **about*** and only set goals that add value to your life.

10. *Set milestones*

    Milestones are the stepping stones needed to help you achieve your goals. For example, if your goal is to lose fifty pounds, what steps do you need to take to help you achieve this goal? If you focus on completing those steps, the goals take care of themselves. In this example *health* is the priority, losing fifty pounds is the goal and the milestone could be to lose two pounds a week via exercise and meal management. The more detailed the milestones are the better your chance of completing your goal. Don't forget to utilize your calendar to mark deadlines for these milestones to help you keep pace and maintain accountability.

Seven Tips for Managing Your Goals

If you only set goals without managing them, failure is imminent. Setting goals requires continuous management for success. Below are seven tips to help you better manage the goals you have now judiciously thought through and set:

1. *Keep goals front and center*

   Make sure tasks associated with your goals are noted on your daily to-do list. If they are not in visual sight, the old adage "out of sight, out of mind" applies here. Just like your daily trivial tasks are included on your to-do list, so should the tasks associated with your goals be included on this list as well.

2. *Track your goals*

   You need to track the progress of your goals and give them the utmost priority on a daily basis. Goals are simple to track but most people don't bother. Then one day—surprise—the completion date for the goal is near and you're not ready. You scramble, but it's too late—another failed goal.

   Tracking your goals is a simple process you manage daily. Create a spreadsheet with the following columns (from left to right):

   a. Goal's name
   b. Date set
   c. Due date
   d. Milestones: for each goal with their own due dates
   e. Status: Highlighted in green, yellow or red
   f. Notes: Keep a log of your goal's successes and failures.

3. *Manage your goals via a routine—make it a habit*

   Establish a daily routine that helps you achieve your goals. If one of your major goals is health-related, then your AM or PM routine should include your daily exercise regimen. (More detail on how to create an AM and PM routine to be covered in the next chapter.)

4. *Live life by the 80/20 rule—complete version 1.0*
   As with anything in life, don't seek perfection. Rather than slowing down trying to achieve 100%, take your goal as far as you can go based on its original due date and complete version 1.0. Eighty percent done is better than another incomplete goal. You can always go back later and make it a new goal to take the finished product to the next level (i.e., version 2.0). Get used to wins not failures. Put a stake in the ground and then start the next goal. Possessing a mindset based on accomplishments (not failures) is crucial for success.

5. *Do not multi-task*
   Focus on one task at a time. In fact, research says each time your mind changes from one task to another it slows you down, makes you less effective and, according to shopnutritional.com, it lowers your IQ while working on cognitive tasks.

6. *Continually push yourself*
   There are no easy/magic solutions to hold yourself accountable to completing a goal. The many tips covered in this chapter will assist in this effort, but the bottom line is *success comes from within—how badly do you want it?* You must be willing to push yourself every day to accomplish your goals. Be positive regardless of the obstacles you tackle on any given day—we all have issues that arise. You've got to believe that your life is a business and your well-being is dependent on you achieving these goals. If your life depends on it, you will strategize frequently to motivate yourself to conquer any obstacles that get in the way of you and your goals.

7. *Reward yourself*

   Congratulations you just completed a major goal! Having some sort of reward system is important for two main reasons: (1) it helps you reflect on your achievement and (2) it will motivate you to accomplish more!

Maintaining Balance

The third key area crucial for successful goal attainment is one that is often neglected: Maintaining Balance. Maintaining balance is a huge part in *maintaining* success and happiness, along with other benefits like preventing burnout, anxiety, and depression. As mentioned earlier in this chapter, evenly spacing out your goals within the Four Priorities of Life will help you live a balanced lifestyle.

However, be cautious as life can be very challenging, making it easy to over-emphasize one priority of life and lose sight of the others. For example, one priority we easily lose sight of is *relationships*, as often we take our family for granted. Unfortunately, I found this out the hard way. Early in life I worked around the clock to achieve my career and financial goals causing me to neglect my relationship with God and my family. Eventually, I ended up losing the love of my life. Don't let something like this happen to you!

A Cautionary Tale Straight from the Horse's Mouth

Believe me when I say: focusing on just a few priorities for a prolonged period will eventually catch up with you and take you down. I thought that focusing on the most important priority, which for me at that time was making lots of money, would be the path to success. I felt that in the end the people I cared about would benefit from my success. Although friends and colleagues warned me to slow down and enjoy my time with my beautiful family, I simply would not hear of it.

I was the ultimate workaholic—an unstoppable machine. Nothing or no one could break my resolve. In time, I completely lost sight of what mattered most in life. I abandoned my morals and broke a few serious biblical commandments. I also convinced myself that maintaining balance was overrated. The concept of living a balanced lifestyle and being successful seemed like an unrealistic oxymoron to me. Something had to give if I was to continue my path to success. I ended up sacrificing my spirituality and then eventually my family. All relationships took a back seat, except the ones required for my career to flourish.

I focused on money, power and excitement as I circled the globe several times. The life I led had all the makings of a great movie. Unfortunately, this "so-called movie" nearly had a tragic end with the main character almost killing himself. I lost everything; my family, most of my wealth, and my power. I even found myself confronting my biggest fear of all—being alone. Up until this point in my life, I had never lived alone. But there I was living alone with no friends or family around me. I didn't really know anyone—as I had kept too busy to socialize with others.

Back when I was in a very bad place, death would have surely been the easiest way out. However, rather than taking the easy way out, I fought back and with the help of a few special people and God I survived through the darkest time of my life. I even wrote a book titled: *On Being A Workaholic*, highlighting the importance of focusing equally on the Four Priorities of Life to maintain balance. I had also taken a 360 degree turn by making relationships equal to my other priorities. I brought spirituality front and center along with my children.

The good news is my story had a happy ending. After six long and painful years of being apart from my wife (my everything), she came back to me and we re-married. My journey was truly a remarkable story and it is my hope that it will help others come to their senses before it's too late.

Conclusion—Fulfill Your Dreams

As you can see there's a great deal of effort required to consistently accomplish your goals. However, there is no greater feeling on this planet than accomplishing those goals. It is the single most motivating factor you'll ever need. Once you complete a *major* goal you will never forget it. It's hard to describe in mere words what the feeling is like. It's a kind of euphoria that not only makes you feel invincible but is extremely addictive as well. The level of intensity is relative to the difficulty of the goal. The harder the goal, the stronger the "feeling of accomplishment" will be. I still remember each and every major goal, even the ones I accomplished over fifty years ago!

With Chapter Three under your tool belt, next we dive into Chapter Four, Time Management. This next chapter is crucial to helping you take your goals to the next level, for without management of your time you will be chasing your tail in a circle trying to get everything done in a day. By managing time, you gain a sense of efficiency, clarity, and purpose that helps you keep chugging forward on your path to self-mastery. So, let's not waste another minute and let's start learning how to manage our time more efficiently.

Chapter 4

Time Management

Despite the fact that most individuals consistently waste several hours a day, it doesn't seem to faze them. It's the same old response: "Tomorrow is another day." When things are too comfortable, we tend to coast along forgetting that time is passing us by, oblivious to the fact that we are not accomplishing our goals. We get easily distracted and oh how we make plenty of excuses. Your mind will say things like "I have plenty of time to complete my goals—I'm only twenty years old," or "I still have three months to complete my goal—what's the rush?" The trouble is—that tomorrow comes, and the goal has not been achieved.

Time is your most valuable resource so why not make the most of it? To accomplish this, you must permanently change your mentality toward time. To change a mindset that has been around for eons is no easy task—but it is doable. Begin by engraining in your mind the concept that you're on this planet once and time is scarce. Ask yourself, "why are you squandering away such a limited and valuable resource?" Once your mind feels the urgency of the situation, this will help propel you to the next level.

How to Not Waste Time

You blink and another five years pass you by. What have you accomplished? Let me answer that for you; nothing! Time is your most valuable resource. However, if you are like most people, time controls you rather than you managing time. Rarely do you get everything done on any given day. Have you ever stopped to think why you always run out of time at the end of the day? Again, let me answer that for you! From my thirty years of life-coaching experience, I have found that individuals run out of time during a day due to a lack of discipline in three key areas of time: structure, self-management, and technology use. Read below to see various examples of characteristics under each category that lead to mis-managed time. Do any of these behaviors apply to you?

1. *Structure*
    a. Operating without a to-do list
    b. Not following an efficient AM and PM routine
    c. Working in a cluttered/disorganized environment

2. *Self-Management*
    a. Not being able to say no
    b. Facilitating insignificant and long conversations
    c. Getting distracted by something upsetting that occurred earlier in the day
    d. No sense of urgency—wasting time like there's an abundance of it
    e. Not realizing wasted time equals wasted money
    f. Lounging in bed every morning—hitting snooze

    g. Wasting time pushing past sleepiness during your non-peak performance times

    h. Dwelling on past issues or things that are unchangeable

3. *Technology Use*

    a. Wasting hours at a time with gaming
    b. Texting endlessly
    c. Obsessing over social media
    d. Distracted by the cellular app du jour
    e. Aimlessly surfing the Internet for hours
    f. Watching too much TV

To learn how to not waste time, you must tackle the above three categories to finally get a grip on life and gain a sense of control. Rather than feeling as though you are chasing your life by the tail, you will be able to lead it and have extra time remaining to just unwind. Take a deep breath, relax, and know that life doesn't have to slip through your fingers. Tighten the grasp of your fist and get ready to lead the way!

Live a Structured Lifestyle

Do any of these examples sound familiar? How often have you wasted time looking for your keys because you forgot where you put them rather than establishing a place where keys belong? You had many errands to do and you zigzagged across the city instead of planning how to get the errands done with the least amount of driving. You forgot to pay a bill because you misplaced it. If you're unstructured you will fail in your quest to improve your wasteful ways.

It's time to execute, but before you can move forward you need to get regimented. Yup, just like being in the military where everything is structured and every minute counts. Dictionary.com defines *structure* as a verb, "to construct or arrange according to a plan; give a pattern or organization to." Simply stated: Without *structure* your life becomes chaotic and hence unmanageable. The more structured you are the more efficient you can be. It's the foundation for success. Just like a house has its foundation, you need to institute structure into your life, so you can be efficient. As a general rule of thumb, structure can be broken down to three main essential elements:

1. Establish and follow a to-do list
2. Adhere to an AM and PM routine
3. Always be organized

The odds of success are greatly improved if you do things in a well-planned, structured and prioritized manner. Keep reading to learn more on how to implement the three essential elements of structure into your life.

Establish and Follow a To-Do List

I am often asked, "What should be included in a to-do list?" The simple answer is everything and anything that needs to get done tomorrow. Your to-do list should include daily obligations and tasks that you need to complete, and don't forget to include tasks associated with your goals. I always tell my clients, "If you don't write it down, consider it forgotten." There's always something to do, whether it's house cleaning, going to the cleaners, taking the kids to the park, etc. Everything should be jotted down even your personal and professional obligations; nothing should be left off.

To add to this, keep your to-do list organized with the following additional housekeeping rules. Make sure all items that must get done that day are highlighted on your to-do list, so they stand out (i.e., I like to circle the most important ones). Also, obligations associated with your goals should be kept front and center; consider making a separate section on your to-do list for these so they don't get lost in your daily tasks. Most importantly, remember the saying, "out of sight, out of mind"? To help prevent this from happening, keep your to-do list with you wherever you go. This way as new things come up throughout the day—you have your list handy to add them on.

With that said, please don't forget a to-do list should be prepared the night before. It's important to be *consistent* with your to-do list and create one daily. Get in the habit of doing this religiously, including Saturday and Sunday. Although there are many apps that facilitate to-do lists, I prefer to document my list on an 8.5 x 11 legal pad of paper in ink and then cross each completed item off with a black sharpie. It feels awesome to visually see items crossed off throughout the day!

Adhere to an AM and PM Routine

A routine is a prescribed, detailed course of action to be followed regularly in the morning when you first wake up (AM) and in the evening a few hours before you go to sleep (PM). Keep it simple. The more complex it is, the more difficult it will be to follow, and you probably won't for very long. Also, no matter how great you believe your memory is, always document your routine on paper until it becomes a habit.

The (Critical) AM Routine

Waking up with a purpose—starts with an AM routine. It's important to hit the ground running without having to think about what to do next, especially when you're trying to clear the cobwebs in the morning. Establish a simple routine—especially for the first few hours of each morning, perhaps something like:

- 0500-0505: Wakeup
- 0505-0515: Wash face, brush teeth, restroom, brew coffee
- 05:15-0530: Recite prayers
- 0530-0600: Review email, drink coffee, eat a small snack
- 0600-0650: Work on projects or goal-related tasks
- 0650-0700: Drive to health club
- 0700-0800: Exercise
- 0800-0810: Drive home
- 0810-0830: Shower and dress for work
- 0830-0845: Drive to work

This routine is obviously for someone who doesn't have to care for a young child. Your morning routine must be individualized to you; it could be longer or shorter than this, but it will define what you need to kickstart your day to help ensure maximum efficiency and energy.

Also, recall from the last chapter we discussed the "Four Priorities of Life." Addressing as many of these priorities in the first few hours of each day will help you gain a strong sense of accomplishment, which will set the tone for the rest of the day. The following are a few examples:

1. Finances: Reviewing your credit card charges daily
2. Career/Business: Checking work related email
3. Relationships: Spiritual responsibilities
4. Health: Exercising, eating a healthy breakfast

As an aside, it's important to include exercise in your AM routine. Exercising daily (especially in the morning) sets the energy level and positive mental outlook needed for a productive day. Whether, it's cleaning your apartment, a walk around the block, going to the gym, or washing the car, it is important to do some sort of activity *every* day.

Finally, the key is to create a routine that you can use every day of the week. Do pretty much the same thing every day with some modifications for anticipated needs. For example, if you need to catch up on your sleep over the weekend or simply relax for a few hours, have a modified routine for Saturday and Sunday.

The PM Routine

Your success during the day is often determined by the discipline of your preparation the evening prior. If you wait until the morning to prepare for your day, you are much more likely to be affected by time pressure and distractions. By knowing what you need to do ahead of time and preparing all of the necessary tools to be used in executing those tasks, you overcome the hurdle of preparation early, leaving your energy and mind free to tackle the steps that count.

Every builder knows that selecting the right material and getting it to the job site is the most difficult part of any construction project. Once everything is in place, the actual execution of building the structure is fun and rewarding. If the material is scattered, misplaced, or missing, a simple job can become a nightmare for even the most experienced professional. Keep your evening routine simple. Below is an example of an evening routine:

- 2000-2015: Prepare lunch for the next day
- 2015-2030: Ready tools needed for the next day—i.e., computers, phones, equipment, literature, research materials
- 2030-2045: Clean dishes and kitchen after dinner
- 2045-2100: Reply to any critical work-related requests
- 2100-2110: Floss, brush teeth
- 2110-2120: Lay out work clothes and workout clothes for the next day
- 2130-2200: Go to sleep

In addition, the following are a few tips that can help you create and support the discipline you need before going to bed:

1. *Set an evening alarm*
   Perhaps on your mobile device to alert you to begin your PM routine in a timely fashion so you go to bed approximately the same time every night.

2. *Clean up your workspace*
   Beginning with a clean and organized workspace in the morning is the most critical shield against disruptive thoughts, tasks, and interruptions.

3. *Create a nightly journal*
   Reflect on the progress of the day and determine what you did well and what could have been done differently. This is best done on paper in a designated place. By keeping track of

your day's progress, you learn to hold yourself accountable. It keeps you focused on objective results, rather than on the amount of time you spend doing any particular thing. Lastly, it creates a written record that can be referenced for motivation, creating a nice way to track the development of your goals and progress.

4. *Make a to-do list*
   We are all groggy when we first get up and it takes a while to clear those cob webs. Therefore, without a to-do list you're inefficient right out of the gate. Don't wake up empty-handed, unprepared and of course not having a good reason to wake up. Always prepare a to-do list the night before.

By following an evening routine, it sets the tone and becomes the catalyst for your morning schedule, which is the most important part of the day. Remember, if you don't follow a good evening routine the odds of you getting out of bed with urgency and executing efficiently throughout the morning are slim to none.

Be Organized

Your work and home environments need to be clean and clutter-free at all times. That includes, but is not limited to, your home, desk, email and car:

- Make your bed as soon as you wake up—if you don't do it first thing in the morning it probably won't get made that day.
- Nothing should be on the floor—your clothes are put away each morning.

- Make sure the dishes are washed each evening.
- Your desk should only have an in-basket and an 8.5x11 pad of paper as your to-do list, oh let's not forget a picture of your family.
- Your drawers should always be organized.
- Your email inbox should be well maintained—fewer than five emails before calling it an evening. These are typically pending items that need to be addressed the next 1-2 days.
- And let's not forget how good it feels to drive in a clean car versus a dirty one!

The more clutter you have in your view, the more clutter you will have on your mind and as a result, the less productive you will be. The more organized you are, the less time you waste both physically (i.e., looking for things you need) and mentally (trying to figure out what to do next). The less time you waste, the more productive you are—it's that simple!

You're Running out of Time—Manage Yourself

The second key area of time is management of yourself. I will never sugar-coat the effort involved to effectively manage yourself. It's a full-time job. Your objective is to be consistently productive. That's not easy considering people are always competing for your time. You have no choice but to focus on yourself first before engaging with others. Fortunately, self-management is a set of skills that can be developed over time. Managing yourself is crucial to be able to manage your limited resource—time. Below are seven important tips on how to better manage yourself. Please stop the waste, before it's too late!

Seven Tips on How to Manage Yourself to Utilize Time Efficiently

1. *Learn to say no*

   In real life your colleagues, friends and extended family love to talk about their issues. They can offer such distractions as irrelevant conversations, personal drama or obsession with detail. If you try to help everyone and take on too much, you will surely fail. Make a conscious decision to balance your time between relevant information and trivial nonsense. If you're not rude and remain respectful, no one will be offended if you cut them off politely. It's all about balancing and prioritizing your time. You have to remember no one else will accomplish your goals; only you can.

   Learn to say no without using the "N" word. You have no choice if you expect to accomplish all of your goals. This is reality. Below are some tips on how to shut people down in the appropriate manner:

   a. *Make excuses (little white lies)*

   Blame it on work, spouse, kids, etc. anything to end the conversation and continue with your daily activities. For example, your boss unexpectedly announced a mandatory meeting that you need to prepare for ASAP.

   b. *Set an Internal time limit*

   Sometimes you have no choice but to listen to someone. In this situation it helps to set an internal five-minute time limit before introducing a white lie to end the discussion.

c. *Speed along their conversation*
Help them get to the punch line of any discussion. Cut detail-oriented people off politely. Constantly interrupt them in a nice way. Even if you're not 100% sure on the point they're trying to make, interrupt and guess (in a polite way). If you're wrong, they will tell you. If you're right—end of discussion.

2. *Don't worry about things you can't control—especially the past*
Why waste precious cycles of time on the past, when there's nothing you can do about the situation. Whether it's the bad investment you made, costing you a lot of money, or an ex-boyfriend who dumped you, there's nothing you can do about it. Worrying about these situations only wastes valuable time. The objective is to look forward and not waste time. It's over, put things behind you and focus on the future. Life must go on—the sooner the better.

3. *Don't sit around wasting time*
Every minute counts, especially when you're trying to get ahead of the game and accomplish more in life. Twenty or thirty years ago, there wasn't as much pressure to do so much in such little time. In most instances there was a lack of urgency. Today, times have changed most likely due to the incredible pace of technology, corporate competition, or the economy. Whatever the reason, the era of doing more with less is here to stay. You no longer have the luxury of siting around and doing nothing. The following are a few tips to help you make the most of your time when waiting:

a. Waiting at the doctor's office or the mechanic's shop: Always be prepared. Bring along your work—whatever that may be. If there isn't a long wait—so be it, you haven't wasted any time and are always prepared if they're behind schedule. Even if you don't own a laptop, grab a book you've been wanting to read. You can even start writing a book, do your school work, or just bring along a pad of paper to take some notes of tasks you need to get done or think of more creative ways to complete your goals ahead of schedule.
b. When you're stuck in a useless meeting: Look attentive but focus on your own agenda. Bring a notepad or one of your work assignments (perhaps something that you can print out). Make sure you sit in the back of the room or close to it. You can also bring your laptop to work on a project—ensure you look at the speaker occasionally, so it seems as though you're taking notes from the meeting.
c. At the airport waiting for your flight or sitting on the plane: Sitting there just looking around is a complete waste of time. Bring writing or reading material.
d. Don't sit in commute traffic (if avoidable):
   i. Get up early and avoid the traffic.
   ii. Get to work early—if management allows it and you don't have any family obligations in the morning.
   iii. Go to a gym close to work—workout first (avoiding traffic), then go to work.
   iv. Stop in a coffee house near your office and do some work on your laptop.

4. *Extrapolate wasted time*

   It's not how many hours you waste a day, it's how many days, weeks and months you've wasted over the course of the year. Your resources are scarce and your mind should be trained to abhor waste. One of the most effective ways to manage your time is to extrapolate wasted time throughout the year. On average people waste four hours a day which, if extrapolated over a year equates to two months of your life flushed down the toilet. Once you realize the waste it will shock you, maybe even scare you enough to *stop the waste* and value time.

5. *Equate time to money*

   Your time is valuable. How much is it worth? Associate an hourly price tag for your time. It's an eye-opening experience.

6. *My brain is tired—but you don't have the luxury of taking a nap*

   I work from home and occasionally when I'm tired my productivity stalls, especially when I'm sitting in front of the computer for hours at a time. Don't try and push it. Get up and do some physical activity i.e., wash the dishes, organize the office, do laundry, etc. Once you get the blood flowing, then go back to the computer and be productive again.

7. *Manage energy for peak performance*

   Some people are more productive in the evening; others are more productive in the morning. Whichever works best for you, perform brain-intense activities (i.e., writing a book or working on a major project for work) during your most productive hours and do less brain-intense activities (i.e., administrative functions, washing dishes, doing laundry, etc.) when you're not at your peak. If you force brain-intense activities when you're tired, the effort will take twice as long and the result will be sub-par.

Interestingly, time management is probably the *most* overly used phrase in the self-help industry. Whether it's time management seminars, training sessions, advertisements for paraphernalia (i.e., expensive planners), numerous books, or thousands of articles and blogs, there's plenty of content out there to teach you time management techniques. Unfortunately, there is very little guidance to help you better manage yourself (as noted above). My focus starts with you! Remember, the better you manage yourself, the more efficient you will become with your time. So, stay positive and focus on the tips above.

Technology Alert: All Circuits are Busy

Finally, we come to the third key area of time: technology. Without discipline, technology sucks us dry, costing us a huge chunk of time without us even realizing it! To make things more complicated, technology can be your biggest ally, or it can be your worst nightmare. Not only is technology popular and widely used, it literally permeates your life, changing your viewpoint as well as your family dynamics. The problem occurs when technology is overused, which causes a sedentary lifestyle and affects your emotional and physical well-being. This new-age of addictive behavior is wasting your livelihood in the *now*. As opposed to utilizing your time thinking strategically for personal and professional development, you're pre-occupied by your devices and the virtual world you access.

Being distracted by technology a majority of the day is a recipe for failure. Keeping this in mind, one wonders, "why are so many people addicted to technology?"

1. *Depression*
   There are many studies that mention people who spend a prolonged period of time on technology do so to escape their own depression. However, rather than helping the depression, technology overuse can be the cause of unhealthy emotions. Instead of going out to meet friends, exercising, seeing family, etc., exorbitant technology use increases loneliness. Thus, worsening the vicious cycle causing you to sit at home alone becoming a victim of your own thoughts.

2. *Boredom*
   According to numerous studies, two thirds of Millennials are bored leading to the excess loss of time on technology.

3. *The fear of missing out*
   This is totally absurd, but many people worry they will miss out on something important, so they become slaves to their phone. They text and check their favorite social media platforms non-stop (i.e., while in bed prior to sleeping or even when in the bathroom).

4. *Ego-driven*
   Society is obsessed with propping themselves up rather than connecting socially with others. These persons end up updating their status continuously along with tagging themselves in pictures to show off.

5. *Feeding their low self-esteem*
   This stems from the mentality that the more "online" connections (i.e., views, followers, likes, friends, etc.) a person has the better off they are in life. This type of person compares their own strengths, abilities, and weaknesses to others to increase their self-esteem.

6. *Lack of discipline*
   Without discipline to manage yourself, you have no accountability and get lost in your technological world.

…And for what? Temporary relief, relaxation or pleasure? There's nothing wrong with having fun, as a matter of fact we all need it. Unfortunately, most of you are not disciplined enough to control your usage and manage your time. The more time you waste on the Internet or watching too much TV, the less time you have for *building the best version of you*. What a waste of life! In fact, according to a Globalwebindex.com 2019 study, individuals waste over three hours a day utilizing social networks and Messaging.

How many goals have gone to the wayside because of this addiction? It irks me to watch people waste so many hours a day on such nonsense. I feel like this addictive behavior is handcuffing so many of you to your technology. Rather than focusing your God-gifted talents and limited resources on accomplishing your goals, all of your circuits are busy. Below are nine tips on how to overcome this technology addiction.

Nine Tips of how to Overcome Technology Addiction

1. Acknowledge your addiction. You know whether or not your addicted.

2. Maintain a journal to see how much time you're spending online. It just may shock you into cutting back.
3. Choose healthy alternatives that get you out of the house more often: go for a walk, bowl with friends or even watch an uplifting movie.
4. Develop yourself (personally and professionally). Isn't that why you're reading this book? Focus on accomplishing your goals versus wasting all of these hours a day on nonsense.
5. Regulate your texting, emailing, gaming, Internet surfing, social media accounts and establish rules:

   a. Never check your apps before going to bed. Research states it affects your mind and will prevent you from going to sleep at a decent hour.
   b. Put your phone away when eating meals, driving, or exercising.
   c. Determine the amount of time you will dedicate to technology use per day.

      i. Who will hold you accountable? Let's be realistic, to date you haven't been able to control your usage. Find a friend or family member to help you.
      ii. Schedule specific times during the day to check your accounts.

   d. Stop posting everything you do. Enjoy the moments and enjoy the people and circumstances that surround you.
   e. Block people that post too much.
   f. Limit the number of social media accounts you have to the ones that are important for business and your personal life.

g. Don't leave apps open in a web browser tab all the time.
6. Block the Internet temporarily using software like Self Control (selfcontrolapp.com) or Freedom (freedomapp.us).
7. Deactivate all of your accounts. Also, remove these apps from your cellphone to avoid the temptation. It's important you don't see the apps on your home screen. You can even change the passwords and turn your accounts over to a close friend or family member.
8. Set a goal of going 21 days without social media. That's how long it typically takes to form a new habit.
9. As a last resort, seek help from a therapist trained in this area and/or support groups.

Although I paint a gloomy picture regarding the addiction to technology, it has many great benefits such as: global connectivity, improved communication, higher levels of productivity, social media apps galore, e-commerce platforms and an unlimited ability to research like never before. Utilizing this powerful technology as a catalyst to be productive and efficient is a great thing, but unfortunately due to your undisciplined mannerisms your bad habits trump the benefits at this time. Learn to control your technology usage now, gain discipline, and then you can better tap in to the pros of technology that await you.

Conclusion—If We Only Had a Time Machine

How great would it be to have a time machine! Not the type that takes you into the past or into the future, but rather one that spews out an unlimited number of minutes giving you ALL the time in the world! Until such a miracle comes into existence, we have no choice but to make the most of the time we have.

By focusing on the three key areas of time discussed in this chapter, you are on your way to learning how to maximize the time you have to get things done each and every day. This means living a structured lifestyle, developing your self-discipline to better manage yourself, and harnessing the power of technology in an effective (self-policing) manner. With these three areas under control, you are one BIG step closer to gaining the self-discipline needed to attain self-mastery. Trust me, you are getting there in a big way.

In the next chapter: Manage Your Sleep, I tackle one of the most time-abused areas. On average individuals waste one to two hours a day not managing their poor sleeping habits. Extrapolate that wasted resource for 365 days…you get the picture. This is why managing your sleep needed to be in the spotlight.

Chapter 5

Manage Your Sleep

(Before, During and After)

Why did I decide to make the topic of sleep a separate Principle? As a teen I set many aggressive goals and according to my mentor he told me: "If I wanted to accomplish that many major goals something had to give—there aren't that many hours in a day to accomplish all of them—you're not being realistic."

As I reached my twenties, I realized he was spot-on. Since I wasn't about to eliminate any of my goals, and I felt that I was efficient throughout the day and evening, I went back to my mentor and asked him what else can I do to accomplish more? He said, "you need to cut back on the number of hours you sleep and to stop lounging around in bed snoozing." But I only sleep eight hours a day during the work-week and perhaps nine to ten hours on weekends and I only hit the snooze button twice. He said, "stop the snoozing and cut your sleep back by one hour each day and take those thirty hours you gain back each month and apply them directly to your goals." That's when my life changed for the better. I eventually began managing my sleep and reduced the number of hours I slept. This was truly a life-altering move.

Here comes my legal disclaimer:

I am not a medical doctor and I am offering my own life experience only as information for you

I tackled the problem by reducing the amount of time I slept by thirty minutes every ten days. I also would pace myself during the day so that I did brain intensive activities in the morning when I was most alert. I also exercised every morning and trained my mind by repeating phrases (self-hypnosis) telling myself I didn't need much sleep. I was able to get my body used to functioning on four hours a night. I did this forty years ago!

Managing the number of hours, you sleep also helps you keep up with family obligations and the myriad of projects and tasks in both your professional world and personal life—something will have to give. Even if you're disciplined and highly productive you will need to cut back on your sleep. Your duties aren't going away and as you mature and support a family the obligations will only increase. It's important to manage your sleep. The bottom line is stop taking your sleep for granted and manage it!

Manage it or sleep your life away

What does it mean to manage your sleep? Managing your sleep encompasses your behaviors *before* you go to sleep, the quality of your sleep *during* the night, and how quickly you get out of bed *after* waking up. Based on my experience as a life coach, I know firsthand that the number of people who manage their sleep is quite low (less than 1%). Unfortunately, this is a huge mistake. You waste an enormous amount of time not managing your sleep etiquette. While we can't do much to alter the quality of our sleep "during" the night, if we tackle it before and after, sleep management automatically improves "the during" sleep. The following are some common mistakes done before and after waking up from sleep:

- Not following a structured evening and morning routine
- Talking to a friend late at night
- Engulfed in social media or gaming late at night
- Being disorganized
    - Having a cluttered room/home
    - Having a cluttered mind

- Lounging around in bed too long every morning because you don't have a morning script (routine + to-do list)
- Over-sleeping due to boredom, depression or lack of purpose
- Pounding your snooze button for up to thirty minutes every day
- Living an unhealthy lifestyle (i.e., eating junk food and not exercising)

And you wonder why you never have enough time to finish your obligations and projects…forget about your goals.

To improve your odds for attaining your goals, you absolutely must manage your before and after sleep habits, which consists of adhering to a disciplined evening and morning routine. If you manage your sleep effectively imagine someone giving you an extra one to two hours a day to invest into achieving your goals. Extrapolate that each month—how would you like to live thirteen months a year? The possibilities are endless with all of that extra time utilized efficiently. So why do some people still sleep more than eight hours per night? From my experience, I believe that depression and boredom are the main culprits. In fact, one of the signs of depression is excessive sleep. It's not that extra sleep is necessary; it's more likely that sleeping through a difficult time is easier than facing reality. It provides an escape from life. If life isn't fulfilling, then we get bored. But if you're passionate about your purpose in life, then in the morning you jump out of bed looking forward to experiencing another day to its fullest.

Most of us don't think about the fact that more than one-third of our life is spent in bed—sometimes sleeping up to ten hours. Do you really need that many hours of sleep? Are you actually sleeping restfully or simply lying-in bed counting sheep? These are important questions to answer to optimize your time and not waste a minute of it. As you lay in bed too long or unable to sleep, realize you are wasting time and falling further and further behind with all of your responsibilities and goals. Now I'm not asking you to cut back the number of hours you sleep at a cost to your health, but what I am asking is for you to take some time and learn how much sleep your body truly needs to maintain a healthy and balanced lifestyle.

In fact, there are two schools of thought out there on this subject in terms of productivity. One group feels you need to cut down the number of hours you sleep to increase your productivity, regardless of anything else. While the second group requires at least eight hours of sleep per night for healthy living. Me, on the other hand, I believe in balance and individuality. Each person is unique. What I ask of my coaching clients is to learn the "minimum" number of hours their body truly needs to function effectively and maintain a healthy and productive lifestyle. While at the same time remembering that if for one reason or another you cannot sleep, even if you haven't hit your pre-determined sleep quota, get out of bed and get working, then take a nap later if needed. You are maximizing the time spent in bed to ensure efficiency and decrease waste which, gives you the pure definition of productivity.

Let's step back and define what sleep is . . . Sleep is the time when your brain and nervous system *rejuvenates* itself. It is also the time your body repairs itself and your spirit connects to higher levels. Below are some fascinating sleep facts:

- Your body has an internal twenty-four-hour clock which controls your *circadian rhythm*. This periodic rise and drop in body temperature tell your mind when to feel tired and when to feel more awake. As body temperature rises, we tend to feel more awake and our brain waves are usually higher. As body temperature drops, we tend to feel more lethargic, tired, and lazy–this is a big cue for our minds to lower brain waves.
- Most adult humans are naturally wired for sleeping twice every twenty-four-hour period–six-to-seven-hour nocturnal rest with a twenty-to-sixty-minute siesta in the afternoon.
- One of the greatest expenditures of energy in the body is from *digestion of food*. Large amounts of blood flow are directed toward the digestive system after a large meal. This means less blood flow, thus less energy, available for the brain. Low blood flow in the brain during sleep means poor sleep quality, since the brain conducts all sleep processes. So, eat light in the evening.

- Your brain cycles through the different stages of sleep, oscillating between deep sleep, and light/REM sleep at a period of about ninety minutes.
- Darker sleep increases melatonin which increases sleep quality and promotes good health.
- Deep sleep is very important for cognitive performance. A lot of "neural housecleaning" occurs during deep sleep, which makes it so important for mood, performance, motor skills, productivity, and creativity.
- During deep sleep your cerebral cortex—the consciousness part of your brain—nearly shuts off. Neural activity in the cerebral cortex breaks down into little islands that can't talk to one another.
- If you go to sleep stressed out, then your mind and brain will be attempting to deal with the stress and this will act as a strain and you won't get quality sleep.
- If you currently spend less than one hour getting high-intensity light, you're suffering from *light deprivation*! Remember, for your eyes spending the day indoors is the equivalent of spending it in total darkness. The more "darkness" you expose yourself to during the day, the poorer the sleep you'll receive in return.
- Your body temperature drops after a hot bath in a way that mimics, in part, what happens as you fall asleep.
- The tiniest amount of light can disrupt circadian rhythm and your pineal gland's production of melatonin and serotonin. LEDs from alarm clocks and computers, although dim, actually do have a measurable effect on sleep quality.
- The wake-up process occurs via increased blood flow to the brain, which is facilitated by the stress hormones ACTH and

Cortisol. By anticipating a wake-up time we set our internal alarm clock. When the anticipated wake-up time arrives, the brain signals the pituitary and adrenal glands to spike ACTH and Cortisol. And you wake up.
- Meditation improves sleep quality. It reduces interruptions to deep sleep. It does this by reducing Cortisol levels during the day. Cortisol destroys sleep quality.
- Our brains thrive on automation.
- Our brain runs on habits.
- EMF stands for Electro-Magnetic Fields. EMFs are released by electronic appliances that are present within your sleeping environment. EMFs are known to disrupt the pineal gland and interfere with the production of melatonin and serotonin which are essential in promoting good sleeping patterns.
- Our body's natural biological clock has been thrown out of balance because of modern electricity and lighting. Biologically the body wants to go to sleep around 10:00 PM and wake up around sunrise.

Now that you have a general understanding of sleep it's important to know how to manage it effectively.

Nine Tips on How to Manage Your Sleep

Below are nine important tips on how to manage your sleep (before, during and after) effectively.

1. *Change the way you think about sleep*
   "I'm not very productive today; I didn't get my eight to nine hours of sleep last night," I've heard this line countless

times. Who says you need that much sleep a night…some doctor who published an article in a medical journal? From the time I was a youngster, it has continuously been pontificated upon me that if I didn't get at least eight hours of sleep each night I would burn myself out and eventually get sick.

Quality sleep is crucial but excessive sleep and lounging around in bed is a *complete* waste of time. Change the way you think about sleep. Don't be dependent on it, believe that it is a necessary requirement and nothing more. It's a means to an end. I view it as a necessity to accomplish my goals, but in order to achieve *all* of my goals sooner I need to sleep the minimum amount and get out of bed promptly.

When you change the way, you think about sleep and your internal clock will automatically change with it. For example, if you've been waking up early since childhood, you're likely still doing this through force of habit. You've trained your mind and your internal clock is set based on repetition, showing this is a habit that can be learned. In fact, tiredness in itself is a habit that *can* be broken. Therefore, challenge yourself to sleep less. The extra time you gain each day means time to accomplish more.

2. *Sleeping the minimum amount by training your mind*
You want to sleep less but you've read that less sleep decreases cognitive abilities. So, what do you do? There are so many things you want to do and so little time in which to do them. So, what's the answer? One answer is to increase the quality of your sleep while also decreasing the amount of time you sleep.

Sleep is a necessity and requirement but I wholeheartedly believe that the amount of sleep is something you can play with. Tell yourself repeatedly: it's just a number and nothing more and that excess sleep is a waste of time. Train your mind by repeating negative phrases or positive affirmations frequently to drive those numbers down to the bare minimum!

a. *Examples of positive affirmations*

   i. I enjoy deep refreshing sleep that fully rejuvenates me
   ii. I dream creatively
   iii. I need less and less sleep to feel fully refreshed

b. *Examples of negative phrases*

   i. You're a pathetic lazy excuse for a human being because you can't get out of bed promptly
   ii. You're wasting your life away in bed

There is no reason why you can't experiment to find the ideal (minimum) amount of sleep your body needs to function at its optimum level. As long as you feel rested and you're productive during the day, then you know you've got it right. Gradually reduce your sleep by thirty minutes each night and hold it for two weeks. Depending on how many hours of sleep your body has been accustomed to, even such a small change can be aggressive. Therefore, it is important to take it slow and see how your body reacts. Each time I cut back on my sleep I would give my body ample time to ensure I was still being productive. If you are doubtful, give yourself more than two weeks before making further changes.

3. *Maintain a good health regimen*

   An important note: to successfully minimize the number of hours you sleep you need to maintain a good health regimen.

   a. *Cut out the bad habits*

   Do not smoke, drink alcohol or beverages with caffeine at dinner time or later that evening. Lunch time or shortly thereafter should be your last drink with caffeine.

   b. *Exercise consistently*

   Exercise daily. Exercising consistently will build strength and stamina, which is required to cut back on your sleep. Do a mixture of cardiovascular exercise (running, biking, swimming, elliptical machine, etc.) along with weight training.

   c. *Do not exercise late at night as it wakes you up*

   If at all possible, exercise in the morning prior to work or in the afternoon it will help you fall asleep earlier in the evening.

   d. *Eat healthier*

   To assist in your new lifestyle, eat energy-stimulating foods and stay away from junk food. Refer to Chapter Nine.

   e. *Push yourself*

   Increase the intensity of your exercise routine to improve the quality of your sleep.

This type of regimen will improve the quality of your sleep. Therefore, you will need less sleep. I can't stress this point enough! Exercising consistently will give your body the fuel and strength it needs to then be able to cut back the number of hours you sleep (if this is your goal) in a healthy manner. Be persistent and remain patient as it may take several weeks for your body to adjust and not be tired. Cutting back on your sleep will not be easy but, it is doable and the hours gained can go a long way towards accomplishing more goals.

4. *Power Naps*

    I am human and there are days when I need a fifteen-to-twenty-minute power nap. Many companies actually have special rooms for their employees to take power naps. Now that you've reduced the number of hours you sleep; power naps are typically needed a few days a week especially in the afternoon after a big lunch. Twenty minutes is the perfect duration to give you that boost of energy—that second wind. If you sleep too much you will get up groggy and won't be very productive. If you're not at work see if you can find a quiet/cool/dark room and make sure to put your phone in do not disturb mode. If you're driving find a rest area. Do not park on the shoulder of the road. If its nighttime park in a lit area where there's people around but make sure to lock all the doors. If you still get foggy or tired during the day, try the following:

    a. Drink vinegar and honey with your water to alkalize your body
    b. Take antioxidants (Vitamin C, Vitamin E, Alpha Lipoic Acid, etc.)
    c. Increase your mineral intake (dried fruits, seaweed, etc.)
    d. Deep breathing

e. Light stretching
   f. Go to that special place in your mind that makes you happy
   g. Drink water with a splash of lemon
   h. Go for a short walk, really noticing things around you
   i. Green Tea, matcha tea
   j. Take some ginseng

5. *When you can't sleep get up and be productive*
   Sometimes your mind is so full of thoughts that it simply will not quiet down, totally screwing up your plans of getting a good night's rest. We've all been there, watching the clock wide-eyed until about two hours before you have to wake up. It happened to me frequently as my mind was always strategizing. I quit fighting it years ago and learned to just get out of bed. Instead of wasting those hours tossing and turning in bed, get up and start working on your to-do list. I was able to get quite a bit done and even go to the gym (I belong to 24-Hour Fitness). Sure, I was a bit more tired in the afternoon, but that evening I went to bed earlier and slept soundly. Accomplishing a few tasks and going to the gym is much better than lying in bed watching precious time waste away.

6. *Be disciplined in the evening—follow your PM routine*
   Try the following simple steps to create the discipline you need before going to bed:

   a. *Prepare your clothes and tools*
      For work and exercise. Do not wait until the morning to try and find the clothes you would like to wear. Also prepare any tools you may need for your profession.

b. *Prepare your lunch (if applicable)*

c. *Clean the kitchen (especially those dirty dishes).*
   Don't go to bed with a messy kitchen.

d. *Create your to-do list—Drain your brain*
   Don't try and sleep with your mind cluttered with things to remember to do in the morning. Always *drain your brain* in the evening. We are all groggy when we first get up and it takes a while to clear those cob webs. Therefore, without a to-do list you're inefficient right out of the gate. Don't wake up empty-handed, unprepared and of course not having a good reason to wake up. Always prepare a to-do list the night before. This will allow you to wake up and hit the ground running with a sense of purpose for the day.

e. *Maintain a nightly journal (optional)*
   Reflect on the progress of the day and determine what you did well and what could have done differently. This is best done on paper in a designated place. By keeping track of your day's progress. It keeps you focused on objective results, rather than on the amount of time you spend doing any particular thing. Lastly, it creates a written record that can be referenced for motivation, creating a nice way to track the development of your goals and progress.

7. *Winding down and relaxing*
   It's important to have a good winding down system.

   a. Stay away from technology

b. Create an optimal environment. Keep your room dark and set the temperature somewhere between 65-68 degrees Fahrenheit
c. Meditate and/or say your prayers
d. Eat a light high protein snack
e. Decrease your intake of liquids
f. Read that book—you'll fall asleep in no time
g. Do something that makes you happy
h. Create a routine that works for you
i. *Legs up the wall in Yoga*

This is one of the best methods to relax. It brings relief to your legs, feet, spine, and nervous system. It is a gentle way to bring the body into a state of deep relaxation and renewal. See https://www.yogaoutlet.com/guides/how-to-do-legs-up-the-wall-in-yoga/

8. *Stop hitting the snooze*

It's the same old routine, nothing ever changes. Unfortunately, it's not that easy to stop hitting the snooze button when your mind is telling you, *"Another ten minutes won't hurt."* The following tips will help you counteract this thought process:

a. *Wake up without an alarm clock*

Be your own alarm clock—it works. If you tell yourself that you need to get up at 6:00 AM your body will start waking up naturally around that time. If you're nervous have a backup alarm clock set for 6:10 AM—just in case. When you start going to bed around the same time each evening you will start to get up without an alarm clock at around the same time each morning. It's all about being disciplined the prior evening. The more structured you are the easier it will be to wake up on your own without an alarm clock.

b. *Move your alarm clock*
Make sure your alarm clock is somewhere out of arm's reach. The farther the better—so you have to walk a few steps.

c. *Have multiple obnoxious alarm clocks*
Ensure your alarm clock spews out a loud and obnoxious sound that you cannot ignore! If loud sounds aren't enough to make you get out of that warm and comfortable bed, then have a second alarm clock in the bathroom or the opposite side of the room. Better yet, ask a friend or family member to hide the alarm clock to really get you going in the morning.

d. *Extrapolate wasted time*
Train your mind by extrapolating wasted time (from snoozing) throughout the year. You will shock your system when you see how much time you're actually wasting and ignite a fire within.

e. *Make it easier to wake up—let the sunshine in*
If you have to get up when the sun rises, it's much easier to do so if you're blinds are open and the sunlight flows in freely. It is much more difficult to wake up if your room is totally dark, especially if you didn't get much sleep that night. Of course, this is predicated on whether or not it is

safe for you to leave the blinds open and what time you are supposed to get up.

Hitting the snooze button should no longer be an option in this day and age when we are all expected to be more productive. It does not do you any good to waste ten to thirty minutes every morning snoozing.

9. *Why stay up*

If you're tired—go to sleep. Even if it's not bedtime. If you stopped being productive hours ago and you've relaxed a bit for the evening—go to bed. Get a good night's rest and recharge your most valuable assets (mind and body) for battle the next day. The worst thing you can do is fight the urge and watch just one more TV show, which wakes you up again and now it's 3 AM and you still can't fall asleep and all for some mindless television.

I do realize that in these days of intense demand on time, that many people are trying to find more hours in the day. Look over these many suggestions and see if by implementing some of them you can both improve the quality of your sleep and reduce the number of hours you sleep. What if you don't want to reduce the number of hours you sleep? By following these tips on how to improve the quality of your sleep, you will have more energy and be more productive during the time you are awake. If you want to get creative, you can experiment with lucid dreaming or learning while you sleep. Below is some additional information on sleep that you may find useful to improve the quality of your sleep.

1. *Things you can do during the day that will improve your sleep at night*

    a. Maintain a positive attitude
    b. Make sure you're regular
    c. Drink lots of water

2. *Things to avoid in the evening*

    a. Arguments
    b. Watching the news
    c. Anything upsetting
    d. Technology

3. *De-stress before going to sleep*

    a. Practice deep rhythmic breathing
    b. Practice EFT on any distressing things that occurred during the day (EFT stands for Emotional Freedom Technique, find out how to do this at www.emofree.com—an easy-to-use de-stressing technique)
    c. Think of three things you are grateful for
    d. Forgive the people who upset you that day
    e. A warm bath (adding Epsom salts and lavender oil or sea salt)
    f. Soothing herbal tea (sleepy time)
    g. Melatonin
    h. Magnesium
    i. Light stretches
    j. Take some probiotics such as yoghurt or kefir

4. *Make your bedroom a sanctuary*

   a. Find sheets that feel good on your skin
   b. Find colors that comfort. Have a picture that you enjoy looking at
   c. Reduce noise and light
   d. Remove EMF fields such as TV, clock radios, cable boxes, etc.
   e. Make the space really dark
   f. Wear a sleep mask
   g. Play soothing music to sleep to
   h. Get an ionizer or humidifier to improve the air quality of your bedroom
   i. Sleep on a comfortable mattress
   j. Visualize a beautiful place that you can go to for relaxation and peace

5. *Think of things you have to look forward to the next day*

   a. A friend you will see or talk to
   b. Something creative
   c. A time with a pet
   d. Time with nature
   e. Something about work that you enjoy

6. *Set Up Rewards for Your Body*

   a. Food
   b. Exercise
   c. Sex
   d. Any sensory pleasure

What you are doing is giving your mind, spirit and body something to look forward to; so that you are reaching to wake up as opposed to dreading it? Hopefully these tips on how to manage your sleep will provide precious time to be more productive every day.

Conclusion—Sleep Right—Sleep Tight—Accomplish More

Just think if you simply had an extra hour each day to do what you want. That extra hour will allow you to accomplish so much more than you ever thought possible. The fact that you gave up your sleep for it makes it that much more sacred. I guarantee you'll make the best of that additional time. When people ask me "Wouldn't you like to sleep a few extra hours?" My response is always the same: *I will sleep plenty when I die.*

There is so much I could write about sleep but there are already hundreds of publications on the subject. My main objective for writing this chapter is to give sleep management the attention it deserves.

In the next chapter we move on to gaining financial discipline. Let's be realistic, if you don't manage your finances, you won't be able to survive in this world. In fact, financial discipline helps you gain the mental and physical freedom you need to better focus your mental energies on mastering your life. The earlier you start, the better off you are . . . so without further ado…advance your token to GO, collect $200 (if only life were a Monopoly game!) . . . and let's get started!

Chapter 6

Focus on Your Finances

When I was in my teens, my mentor kept telling me: "Your priorities should always be *money*, *gym* (*health*) and *sex*. Never deviate!" The first time he mentioned those words I was confused—I also thought he wasn't really serious. Afterall, I was a healthy teen with raging hormones! I told him you know that's impossible, right? He said, "If you meet your financial obligations; make and save as much money as possible, be frugal throughout the day, live by a budget and maintain a good health regimen (cardio and weight training) each morning you will have time for your personal endeavors in the evening." Shouldn't my future family always come first? "As you get older and have children—being financially secure should still be top priority, because without money you can't support your family's needs (education, medical, housing, etc.). Medical issues alone come with a hefty price tag. As I matured, I realized he was right.

The World Revolves Around Money

Money is not the root of all evil as pontificated by so many. Having the appropriate amount of money is peace of mind. Unfortunately, this world revolves around money. Without a good nest egg your relationships are impacted, your health is impacted because you can't visit the doctor, pay for meds, go for exams periodically, etc. and your overall happiness is also impacted because you can't take those wonderful vacations you've always dreamt about or buy that new car you desperately need to replace that broken down clunker. Most people do not manage their finances until it's too late and they have big problems and undoubtedly pay the price (pun intended). Some of the most common issues I have seen with my clients are as follows:

- Accumulating credit card debt
- Not setting achievable financial goals
- Poor bill management
    - Not paying bills in a timely manner—accruing late charges
    - Cumbersome/manual administrative process
    - Misplacing bills
- Not knowing your numbers
    - Unaware of account activities and balances *on a daily basis*
    - Not knowing *exactly* how much you spend on an ongoing basis
- Not being frugal-minded
    - Purchasing unnecessary (nonsense) items on impulse
    - Purchasing the latest technological gadget
    - Spending way too much—living paycheck to paycheck

- No savings
- Making risky decisions with your hard-earned money
- Having only one source of income—keeping all your eggs in one basket
- Poor record-keeping
- Operating without a budget
- Poor financial planning
    - Not investing for the future
    - Not having a Will and/or a Living Trust
    - Not owning a home—paying rent

This is an eye-opening list; do you want to struggle financially until the day you die or would you rather be financially secure and enjoy the fruits of your labor and living life to the fullest? Sure, managing your finances is an effort, but isn't anything worthwhile hard work? It means knowing how much you spend, growing your nest egg, eliminating any bad debt you may have and investing for the future. It's also being organized and paying your bills on time, saying no to spontaneous spending (i.e., eating out often with your friends or going to the tavern too often and always picking up the tab). My fourteen tips below are proven, genuine and simple to follow and will allow you to achieve your financial goals:

- Travel the world
- Spend more time with your family
- Spend more time on your hobbies
- Donate more to charitable causes
- Buy that dream house, boat, car or why not all three
- Pay your children's college tuition without going into debt

For me, managing my finances allowed me to transform myself into a multi-millionaire at the age of thirty-eight (in 1992).

Fifteen Tips to Financial Freedom

Below are fifteen important tips on how to manage your finances effectively and achieve financial security.

1. *Do whatever it takes to eliminate credit card debt*
   Consider your credit card as if it were a demon, a temptation from hell. A credit card invites you to put yourself in debt. It encourages instant gratification and irresponsibility. When you use a credit card, it does not feel like you are spending real money so it devalues what you spend.

   Do *not* buy something if you don't have the funds to purchase it outright. Being in credit card debt is disastrous. Once you do in many cases the amount you owe spirals out of control and the interest rate you will pay on that balance is so ridiculously high. If you are in credit card debt then it should be your top priority to get out of it as quickly as possible. Once you've achieved a zero-monthly balance but if you are not disciplined enough to pay the full amount each month then I highly recommend shredding your credit card. You are allowed one card for emergencies and for things like ordering necessities over the Internet.

2. *Set realistic financial goals*
   If your finances are a mess don't set outlandish goals that you wouldn't have a chance in hell to accomplish. Initially, take baby steps. But before setting goals make sure you document your expenses—all of them, which is the foundation for

creating a budget. Once you have a good snapshot of your expenses then establish realistic goals. Start small i.e., start a savings account and deposit a nominal amount each month or automatically deduct from your paycheck every two weeks.

3. *Establish common goals with your partner*

   If you have a partner, then you should establish common goals. After there is agreement, then you and your partner should discuss how to achieve those goals. Harmony is created when both parties agree on common goals and agree on how to achieve them. Also, it will be important to establish roles:

   a. Who will be responsible for paying the bills?
   b. Who will keep accounts organized for taxes?
   c. Who will monitor bank accounts daily?
   d. Who will monitor credit card purchases?
   e. Who will maintain the budget?

4. *Simplify bill payments*

   I pay my bills automatically via one credit card, which provides me with cash back for every purchase and via my checking account for those vendors who do not accept credit cards. It's important to keep things simple. Using only one or two methods will make managing your finances easier and quicker. Also, for those irregular bills that come in the mail always put them in the same place.

5. *Monitor bank and credit card accounts daily*

   Managing your expenses are just as important as making more money. Unfortunately, most people don't even know how much they spend each month, yet they know how much they earn. Eventually your expenditures will creep up higher and higher and you will be upside down and even go into debt. One of the biggest mistakes people make is *not* monitoring their bank accounts and credit card purchases daily. It's important to know your numbers (i.e., how much you spent on your credit cards and how much is in your bank accounts) and to validate all transactions that were posted overnight. Checking your accounts online daily should be noted on your to-do list so you don't forget.

6. *Pay Your Bills Immediately*
I am frequently asked, "Why should I pay my bills immediately? They're not due for several weeks. Doesn't it make more sense to accumulate all my bills for the month and pay them at one time?" There are no advantages to paying your bills at the end of the month however, there is one huge benefit to paying your bills immediately. One of the biggest advantages is to know your *real* balance as quickly as possible. Once I receive a bill, I typically make my payment within 24-48 hours unless I'm away on business. Let's say your current balance is $5000.00 and you have $4800.00 in bills to pay, waiting until the end of the month may cause you to forget how many bills you've accrued and the total amount owed, which may trigger you to make unwarranted purchases. Knowing the *real* balance in your checking account may cause you to think twice before making purchases you don't need.

7. *Train your mind to always be frugal*
Establish negative phrases that promote an image of going broke. Repeat those phrases several times each day until you

begin emulating this lifestyle. For example: *"In case I lose my job, do I have enough money in my account to support my family for at least one year?"* or you can go one step further and use hard-core negative phrases like: *"I am going to lose my job any day and I won't be able to support my family."* This is my preferred choice, I felt that hardcore phrases were more impactful. It helped me save more by withdrawing additional funds from my paycheck and depositing it directly into my savings account, which meant I had less disposable cash each week for expenditures.

You may argue that the odds of losing your job are minimal, especially if you're a high performer and maintain a good relationship with management. You can also argue that being this negative would cause you to be so stressed out and depressed that you could lose focus on getting the job done in an efficient manner. I was laid off in my prestigious and long IT career—it was a harrowing experience. It had nothing to do with my performance. It had everything to do with the economy and the company closing its doors for good. After the layoff, I wanted to make sure that if it ever happened again, I had a large savings account to support my lifestyle and pay my bills for at least one year. Being negative internally did not change my personality, no one knew the internal war that was brewing, but it made me work harder, smarter and more efficiently to excel in my career and the more I made the more I saved.

Create your own phrases. If you prefer to use positive affirmations then establish phrases that promote an image of being successful by having a hefty savings account. If you train your mind effectively you will be frugal, which means you will question every purchase repeatedly and be very selective about making that purchase.

Train your mind to think that you're barely making enough to pay your monthly bills. The most effective way to help you be frugal is to believe that you're broke. Just telling yourself to manage expenses prudently does *not* work. Below are tips on how to train your mind to manage expenses effectively:

a. *Don't buy the latest and greatest*
Question yourself repeatedly. Do you really need to buy that item right now? You've survived without it all these years. The more you question yourself, the less likely you are to buy it, which means you probably didn't need it to begin with.

b. *If you own a business train your mind to believe the economy will crash any day*
Even in the best of times, because you know eventually everything must come down. You should operate your business like the economy will crash any day. This doesn't mean you stop investing in necessary programs and functions—it just means managing your expenses 365 days a year. It's a big mistake putting sound financial management practices on the back burner during the best of economic times. One of the stupidest things that businesses do is to reduce expenditures only during economic downturns. They have layoffs, curtail spending and ask everyone to do more with less. Why wait until it's almost too late?

c. *Extrapolate expenditures throughout the year*

You don't think about how much you spend on any given day. "What's $5.00 here or a few dollars there…it's all incidental expenses, right?" Wrong—it all adds up. If you don't have a vague idea of how much you spend throughout the year it will sneak up and blindside you but, by then it's too late. Calculate your expenses. For example, how many times do you go out to eat? Let's say you average two outings for lunch in a week at a cost of $10.00 each, and the same number of outings for dinner at a cost of $25.00 each. If you look at it from that perspective you might think it's no big deal however if you forecast it over a month's period = $240.00 per month and even more eye-opening = $3360.00 a year. I'm not saying to cut out the fun in your life (dining out, entertainment, etc.), rather forecast your expenses and see if it fits into your yearly budget, the sticker shock may frighten you enough to start budgeting appropriately. Just limiting your outings to one lunch and one dinner a week will save you $1680.00 a year. That's a substantial savings. Did you just spend double for a movie ticket taking your wife in the evening instead of going to the Saturday afternoon matinee? With the money you saved from evening movies throughout the year, you could buy her a nice gift. Always extrapolate recurring incidental expenses throughout the year—wake up and shock your system.

d. *Stop spending on small insignificant things to save and purchase important items*

If you keep wasting your hard-earned money on nonsense your odds of making those larger purchases like a home, new car, etc. diminishes significantly. Remember managing expenditures, especially the small insignificant stuff, should be given equal attention as your income, savings and investments. There are many ways to be more prudent and help avoid flushing your hard-earned money away. Below are a few examples:

   i. Daily lunch outings quickly become a waste of time and money. Bring your lunch and save precious resources. If you must go out to break up the monotony, then once a week should be sufficient.
   ii. Not picking up the entire tab at the bar for all of your buddies. This is stupid!
   iii. Roll your own coins. Before taking that big jar of coins to the machine at Wal-Mart and paying that hefty fee to automatically count. Roll them yourself while watching a movie.
   iv. Manage utilities:

   - Turn the lights off immediately when leaving a room.
   - Don't leave the shower running while taking a shower. Turn the shower on to wet yourself down, then turn it off while lathering, then turn it back on to rinse thoroughly.
   - Set your AC to somewhere in the 76-78 range in the summer time and your heater no higher than

68 in the winter time. If 68 is too cold where some extra layers around the house
- Don't run your pool pump for eight hours a day, four hours a day is sufficient.
- Don't pay for cable packages not utilized; only purchase what you use.

Being frugal doesn't mean you can't have fun. My daughter and I go out to dinner at least once a week. We don't spend much, a typical bill averages $25.00. We don't purchase beverages. I taught her to avoid ordering drinks from restaurants because that's where most establishments make their biggest profits. The $5.00 + we save on sodas or coffee each week will net us a few hundred dollars at the end of the year, which will allow us to dine out more frequently. If she feels like drinking a soda, we always have a 2-liter bottle of Sprite (her favorite) at home which we bought on sale at Wal-Mart for $1.00.

8. *Train your mind to save and to always beat your previous number*

   It's not only fun to watch your balance grow, it's also *very* addictive. Even if it's a small amount view it daily. After a short period of time, you'll be hooked to saving more. Savings must be a priority. Consistently save and never withdraw funds from your savings account unless it's for an important purchase like a car or home. It should not be used for vacations or purchasing Christmas gifts, it should only be used for *significant* necessities and investments. You should set an amount and deposit those funds into your savings account each time you're paid. Even if you can only save a minimum of $10.00 every pay period, the actions taken to constantly save are more important than the actual balance. Also teach your children how to consistently save. My daughter gets tips from work, typically a few dollars. All coins and bills go into a jar, at the end of the month she rolls up those coins and deposits it into her bank account. That's my little girl!

You should try and increase the amount you're depositing periodically. Perhaps after several months you can increase the amount to $15.00 per pay period, etc. Increasing the amount, you are saving and watching your balance grow feels great and will give you peace of mind. Once you have a substantial amount saved, in case of a major emergency, you will feel like you are standing on solid ground. Saving will become habitual. Your mind will always want to see more—to always beat your previous number. Train your mind (Refer to Chapter One) by conversing with yourself repeatedly, for example:

a. I can't touch this; I have to find another way.
b. This money is *only* for emergencies. Don't touch your savings, an emergency will occur one day and you won't be prepared.
c. Do I want to live in an apartment and pay rent for the rest of my life?

These thoughts may sound harsh but, they will help combat all the temptations you are being subjected to daily.

9. *Be risk-averse*

Do *not* invest in the stock market to make a quick buck. It's for long-term investments. Do *not* get involved with any 'get-rich-quick' schemes. If it sounds too good to be true, then it probably is! Do *not* lend money to associates or friends, odds are 50/50 that you will never see your money again and your friendship will deteriorate or potentially end. You have worked hard to earn these resources; you have a duty to conserve them.

10. *Have multiple sources of income*

    Do not have all your eggs in one basket. If you rely on that one work-related paycheck, it's a formula for a future disaster. The bills will always be there, but your job may not. You should never be satisfied with one source of income in case one dries up. In this Internet business-conducive era it's easier to have a side business or a second job. Never be complacent and constantly strategize for supplementary career and/or business opportunities. The sooner you can achieve a second source of income the better!

    Making lots of money needs to be a priority—everything continuously increases in price (food, gas, education, clothes, rent, etc.) say it dozens of times each day—I need to make more money—never settle!

11. *Keep good records*

    It's crucial to maintain good records throughout the year especially if you own a business. Don't wait until the end of the year and try to make sense of all your undocumented business expenses. Establish a simple spreadsheet and maintain it! If you don't have your own business remain organized and maintain your receipts, especially during tax time.

12. *Establish a budget*

    Create a budget—sure it's an effort but it's well worth it. If you don't know how much you spend throughout the year then how can you manage your resources effectively? A budget is a summary of expected expenses for a certain period of time (typically monthly). Create a simple spreadsheet. Start by first listing absolute necessities—those expenses you have to pay in order to live (i.e., rent, food, transportation, utilities, medications, etc.). Second, don't forget to include the amount deposited into your savings account, as part of your overall expenses. Third, list all of your bills—there are your monthly bills, such (i.e., credit cards, rent, utilities, etc.) and then there are others. Which ones need to get paid? If you have little to work with and have to choose which bill to pay, think carefully of the consequences of not paying that bill. In other words, which bill will have the least impact on me if I delay it for a month? Lastly, if the income required is met to pay all the bills, you can now list the extra things you would like to purchase. These are desirables (i.e., dinner out, a new purse, etc.). Voila! You now have a budget for the month.

13. *Contribute into your company's 401K program*
If offered and you're not in credit card debt sign up for the maximum amount of your company's 401K program it will be a smart, sound and safe investment. If you are in credit card debt you should still take out the minimum amount. It's a good habit to initiate. They are an excellent way to invest, especially for your elder years. Don't rely solely on our government for retirement.

14. *Initiate and maintain a Will and/or a Living Trust*
If you have dependents, no matter how little or how much you own, you need a legal document. Don't think about yourself, think about your loved ones.

15. *Eventually purchase a home*

    Purchasing a home is still one of the best and safest investments despite the collapse of the US housing market in 2008. Only purchase a home if you have enough resources to make your monthly mortgage payments on time. You must also establish an emergency fund (in your savings account) to pay your mortgage payments for at least six months, preferably one year in case you suddenly lose your job.

Conclusion—Manage Your Money or Else Pay a Hefty Price

Striving for financial security will give you the peace of mind we all desire. Financial security begets safety and confidence. If you feel safe and secure about your money, then that gives you power and certainty. If you don't take the time to do it right—manage every aspect of your finances daily (i.e., expense monitoring and management, savings, investments, fulfilling administrative obligations, having multiple sources of income, etc.) you will definitely pay a hefty price in the very near future.

In the next chapter I discuss how to excel in your career as quickly as possible by utilizing my thirteen tips. Also, many of us want to start that side-business while working a 9-5 job. My nine tips help you get that business you've always wanted off the ground.

Chapter 7

Excel in Your Career and/or Business

Whether it's your career and/or business, your work consumes more than one-third of your life—don't you think you should get the biggest bang for the buck and give it the attention it deserves? Afterall for most of you it's your primary source of income. Without that income you can't survive in the world, except maybe in a homeless shelter, but they encourage you to eventually get a job. Having a steady source of income also improves your self-worth. It feels good to have money and being able to purchase items for you and your loved ones. Individuals who are seeking employment approach jobs with differing levels of requirements and eagerness.

Jobs, Careers and Businesses

The three distinct situations are:

1. Some just want a constant paycheck and a simple (no-brainer) 9 to 5 job function.

2. Others search and attain a meaningful career with a bright future in an industry they are enthusiastic about.
3. Certain individuals are in 9 to 5 jobs and want more out of their life, but cannot afford to relinquish that paycheck and invest their time to seek greener pastures (a new career or perhaps a side business).

This variance defines the difference between jobs, careers and businesses. While your job consists of the tasks you perform daily to earn income, your career encompasses all of your experience, prowess, creativity, resourcefulness, commitment, education, discipline and hopefully a roadmap (strategy and action plan) highlighting the path for success within a particular industry that you are passionate about. Below are my thirteen tips for individuals who are in positions with opportunities to excel in their career (Situation #2 from the list above). These tips can be applied to small, medium and large size companies.

Thirteen Tips on How to Excel in Your Career

1. *Superior performance trumps everything*
   Performance warrants top billing. If management sees you as a high-performer they will typically reward you. Bonuses aren't guaranteed, but if your company does handout yearly bonuses your odds are greatly improved. Effective workload management combined with focus on perception, being cautious and proactive with the political landscape improves your odds even further. Below are some tips to help you become a top performer:

a. *Continuously strategize*
   To complete your job responsibilities more efficiently—be resourceful and creative (think outside of the box for better solutions).

b. *Prioritize your workload*
   Focus on the most important tasks/projects first.

c. *Maintain structure*
   Be organized and follow a to-do list.

d. *Work with urgency*
   To complete your tasks and goals on schedule or better yet ahead of schedule.

e. *Be goal oriented*
   Every company sets goals and does whatever is necessary to achieve those goals. It's important that you establish goals based on your job function, which are closely aligned with company goals—manage them to fruition.

A word of caution: Don't over promise and under deliver. Be careful not to mouth off and promise the world and not deliver. The value of action speaks volumes over measly words applies here big-time.

2. *Showcase initiative*
   Employers are looking for individuals who can bring fresh ideas to the table and take initiative to start new projects without being directed to do so, pitch new solutions and create new opportunities for the business. It's going above and beyond your normal job responsibilities. It's also volunteering

to help out in other areas. Work hard, work smart, volunteer for new projects, come up with new more efficient processes, go out of your way to help others.

Come to work early, apply yourself, and don't watch the clock to leave exactly at quitting time. If you really want to excel in your career don't be labeled a 9 to 5 person. Also, don't make personal calls at work, text aimlessly or utilize your social media apps.

3. *Play the political game to survive and thrive*

    I hate the politics in D.C. and I hated playing the political game at work even more. With D.C. politics I could pretty much ignore, but if you don't play the game at work, you will not excel in your career, in many instances, could lose your job. Politics run ramped in every company (small, medium and large). Below are a few tips on how to play the dreaded game:

    a. *Acquaint yourself with the organization chart*

       It's important to know who the key influencers and power players are. Who are the brains in the organization? Who are the most respected? Who are the real decision makers? Also, who to be leery of…

    b. *Assess relationships*

       Be observant to see who the movers and shakers are interacting with—perhaps in a formal group or informal setting. Are there any social networks you need to get involved with? Ascertain if relationships are based on respect, friendship, romance or something else. If at all possible, determine how influence emanates among the different groups. Be cognizant of friction or interpersonal conflicts.

c. *Develop your EQ skills (See Chapter Two)*
It's crucial to communicate effectively with you colleagues and executives also, to manage your emotions.

d. *Be professional at all times*
There's a time and place for fooling around, and it's not the workplace. Acting stupid (i.e., yelling at someone, throwing a tantrum or bad-mouthing someone) doesn't do anyone any good, especially you. You don't want to be labeled as a hot head. Also, don't complain about your workload, no one cares. No matter how good a worker you may be, getting caught in the web of gossip will quickly downgrade your standing with your boss and employer.

e. *Begin building your brand/profile*
In other words, are you someone who gets the job done? Are you trustworthy? It's important to showcase your honesty, integrity and accountability.

f. *Don't toot your own horn*
Let your accomplishments speak for themselves.

g. *Begin building your network*
Start making connections outside of your own team (i.e., co-workers, managers and
Executives). Be friendly towards everyone, however only align yourself with the key players and organizations.

h. *Be positive and friendly*
There are going to be plenty of individuals who practice negative politics. Don't shy away from them but don't go down to their level either. The old adage "keep your friends close and your enemies closer applies here. Be guarded but courteous and respectful. Get to know them and their goals. Just be careful what you say around them as they may take your words and pass it along with a negative spin. Although many of these individuals are insecure and are self-destructive, they are clever and dangerous.

i. *Choose your words carefully*
You don't want to reveal secrets that will be misconstrued. If you want to voice some concerns, be confident but never be aggressive. Also, never bad mouth anyone.

To survive and thrive in the business world you need to be shrewd, observant, and have the gift of gab, just like politicians. Having to embrace the political landscape of any company seems like such a complete waste of time, but to be successful you either play the game and do it well or simply move aside so you won't get trampled by those who are in the game to win. It's that simple!

4. *The right perception speaks volumes*
If you typically work 40 to 50-hour weeks make it appear to upper management that you're working 60 to 70-hour weeks, when in reality you're not. In small, medium or large businesses portraying the right perception is a key success factor to excel in your career. Don't think of it as being deceitful.

Consider it more like battle field tactics to out-maneuver or outsmart the enemy. The following are some tactics:

a. Let's say it's Wednesday and your project is due the following Monday. You should do as much as possible during the work week and even if you finish the project on Friday afternoon you shouldn't email the deliverable just yet—wait until the weekend. Every manager looks at the time stamp on emails that come in during off-hours. Work-related emails you send during these off hours will draw management's attention.

b. It's also a good idea for you to work a few extra hours to catch up in a quiet environment. Early Saturday morning, perhaps before your family or significant other wakes up is ideal. You should send email to management and his team throughout the weekend—if applicable.

c. The same advice goes for status email. You should complete them and place each one in your Draft email folder—then click send in the evening. It appears that you're working around the clock, but in reality, you're not. If you use Outlook, you can also schedule the email to be sent automatically.

d. When interacting with management about a certain project that has been assigned to you with unrealistic demands: As much as you may want to, you should never say no—you should tell management that you will work on it over the weekend and send the deliverable before Monday. You should remind management (subtly) that your current responsibilities will fill up the work-week and you don't want to drop the ball on anything. You shouldn't make it look like you're complaining. It's just a gentle reminder that your plate is full and you will get to this very important project over the weekend when it's easier to complete the work without interruption. You should work on the project and complete as much as possible during the week, as time permits, but not tell your boss and click send sometime over the weekend.

Management will typically recognize you as a company person. They will think that you're working day and night and you're doing whatever it takes to get the job done. Following this simple piece of advice will help your career immensely. Congratulations, you just won a strategic battle.

5. *Be one step ahead of your boss*

    You should never wait for your boss to tell you what to do next. Always anticipate management's needs. Put yourself in their shoes and ask questions like what would they do next to make improvements in the organization? How do we make things more efficient? Which processes or procedures do we need to implement, which will streamline our workflow? Be proactive (i.e., observe, listen and recommend solutions).

6. *Earn the trust of management*

    Every executive has their own method of managing the organization (i.e., hands-on, hands-off, etc.). Do you fit into their management style? You don't have to be best friends with your boss, but you should establish and nurture a solid relationship. Know the way they think and understand their expectations (likes, dislikes, status reporting, deliverables, etc.). The better you get to know your boss the more successful you will be. If you gain the trust of your boss, you will be in good standing. You will probably get better projects, better raises, and more opportunities for promotions.

7. *Know your employer*
   Learn your company's products, services, mission, vision, strategies, goals. The more you know about your company mission, vision and goals the better you can align your work-related goals. Knowing your employer will help you better understand your role and the value you provide to their success.

8. *Ask your boss for constructive criticism*
   In a future one-on-one meeting ask them to be brutally honest and ask what they think of your strengths and weaknesses. Don't wait for your annual performance review. In most instances management will be happy to provide this feedback.

9. *Don't go to management with problems—come with solutions*
   Good employees go to management with solutions not problems. Be a problem-solver not someone who just points out problems. If you don't have the authority to provide the final verdict on a problem, then make sure you offer a few solid options to management and try to help as much as you can.

10. *Increase your knowledge base*
    You should never stop learning new skills. If you do the same thing over and over without learning new skills you will get bored. Whenever your employer offers training courses or other forms of education, jump on the opportunity.

11. Be a team player

At least make it appear that way—especially to management. Below are a few pointers on how to be a good team player:

a. *Be an active participant*
When interacting with individuals and organizations, be an active participant on projects and be sure to say the *we* word repeatedly. Never use *I*. Volunteer for assignments outside of your department and come prepared to team meetings and listen and speak up.

b. *Be receptive to other people's ideas*
Listen and be open-minded on other people's ideas. Solicit feedback on your ideas.

c. *Be reliable*
Always meet your deadlines to earn the trust of your co-workers. Keep your word and deliver quality work. You're counted on to consistently deliver.

d. *Adapt easily, quickly, and be flexible*
To changing situations. Also, never display stress or complain. Take things in stride as things will not always go according to plan.

e. *Be a problem solver*
Great team players are problem solvers. They collaborate with others to find solutions. Sharing information and knowledge is a key component to being a great team player.

f. *Communicates effectively*
Communicates confidentially and frequently with other team members in a respectful manner is common

practice. They're not afraid to speak up but do it in a positive, confident, and respectful manner.

g. *Promote team goals*
The focus is on team goals versus individual goals.

h. *Be humble*
Point out the contributions of others and don't seek attention for your accomplishments.

12. *The first thirty days*

As a new employee you're on management's radar. The first thirty days in a new job are crucial for overcoming any skepticism that's institutionalized in most companies for all new hires. This is why it's important to minimize any uncertainty as quickly as possible and have a positive impact on the organization immediately. Be resourceful and do whatever it takes to learn your job quickly and get it done in a quality manner. Most companies are not going to give you a long time to learn your job and you probably won't have someone shadowing you for a few weeks. If you're lucky you may get a few days of classroom training, a few manuals to review with very little on the job training time.

Establish the appropriate perception immediately—like the first day, by staying past the time you're supposed to get off and always get in early, preferably prior to management arriving on day two. Come in as early as possible even if you don't get paid for it. You will be rewarded later. You need to show management that you're a company person from the get-go. Below are some tips to ensure a great first impression:

a. *Join co-workers for lunch or coffee*
   Even if you don't have the time—you should do it. You need to get acclimated to the team as quickly as possible.

b. *Ask questions*
   You need to ask your co-workers for advice on the do's and don'ts for your first thirty days. Also, about dress code, how meetings are conducted and who are the key players.

c. *Take plenty of notes*
   More importantly, make sure people are seeing you take notes, but don't take notes on your phone during this period.

d. *Be extra diligent not to make a mistake but, if you do, you need to admit it immediately*
   Let management know and also tell them what you will do differently next time.

e. *Don't make waves*
   It's better to keep quiet during the first few weeks—listen and learn.

f. *Adapt to the corporate culture and adhere to departmental values*
   Fit in quickly. Ask questions and observe.

g. *Make it a point to meet with management regularly*
   Especially in the first week, but you need to come prepared with an agenda. Discuss training progress, your 30-day plan, status reporting and management's expectations.

h. *Change email settings to engage spell-check and a one-minute send delay* email is a great productivity tool, but it could also be your worst nightmare. If you're not sure how to articulate an important message—you need to draft something, save it and check it the next morning when you're not brain tired, before sending.

i. *Don't step on anyone's toes*
You may find things in the department that could be performed more efficiently, if that's the case, you need to approach management and start each sentence in this manner:

- "This procedure works well, but I was wondering if you've already tried to do . . . "
- "I am sure this has been tried before, but I was thinking, what if. . ."
- "You guys have been doing this a lot longer than me, but here is a thought. . ."

13. Nurture relationships

The more people you know the better especially with key decision makers or folks who are influential. If you don't *proactively* manage professional relationships, your success in business will be limited. Typically, nurturing key business relationships is taken for granted and put on the back burner which is a huge mistake. Promotions and bonuses are not only based on performance, but, sadly, on who you know. You need to pick and choose relationships with key executives who can contribute to enhancing your career. You need to schmooze those key stakeholders. Those executives that can help catapult your career.

I've known many individuals who struggled in their management career because they failed to schmooze with the appropriate people. As many stated, "I'm not about to kiss anyone's butt." I replied, "Schmoozing was not about kissing someone's butt. In fact, the definition of schmooze is to: *converse informally, to chat, or to chat in a friendly and persuasive manner especially so as to gain favor, business or connections."*

That's a lot to digest but making the most out of your career is crucial. Utilize these career-related tips and you can put yourself on the path to greatness and achieve your ultimate career goals. If you feel like you're in a dead-end job, but there are opportunities all around you in the same company the thirteen tips above will help you change your current situation.

More than half of my clients are looking for a second or third source of income, but they can't put their current job on hold to pursue other interests. Very few have the luxury of quitting their job outright to perhaps start their own business. Unfortunately, there are no magic potions. It will take hard work (working nights and weekends), resourcefulness, creativity and most of all the discipline to ensure accountability, urgency and tenacity to achieve success. You will also need a *product* or a *service* that is unique, valued and cost-effective. So, don't quit your day job just yet, at least until your side business is fully established and profitable. Below are my nine tips on how to bridge the gap between your current 9 to 5 job and establishing another source of income.

Nine Tips on How to Build a Startup Business While Working a 9 to 5 Job

1. *Take your new venture seriously*

   Don't start this venture by thinking it's a part-time gig or perhaps just a pastime. Set the proper mindset by believing it will be your livelihood and it will take hard work. Set goals that are measurable and realistic and just as important, how will you hold yourself accountable to ensure goal compliance? Also, don't kid yourself ... working a fulltime job and establishing a business on the side will be difficult, but it is doable, however *only* if you can manage yourself by making efficient use of nights and weekends. The days of procrastination need to be long gone—making every minute count is your new mode of operation!

2. *Build it so they will come*

   Whether your new business provides services or products, ask yourself the following questions:

   a. Who are your customers?
   b. What are the costs associated with the services or products you are offering?
   c. How will you market your services or products?
   d. What will set your services or products apart from all the other establishments or professionals providing the same type of service or product?
   e. What's so special about your product or service offering?

   These are some of the most important questions to ask yourself. The answers to these queries will be the foundation for your strategy moving forward.

3. *Have a darn good portfolio*

   If your business provides a service, develop and showcase a bio that is unique, depicting your experience, credibility and that you are results oriented. There are many consultants available, you need a competitive advantage to set you apart from the pack.

4. *Authenticate your idea*

   Who doesn't think their idea will be that ONE product that takes off? After coaching dozens of entrepreneurs, every one of them (100%) believe that their idea is unique and incredible. No wonder there are so many businesses started every year. Unfortunately, almost just as many close their doors shortly thereafter. Typically, because products have not been fully researched, undeveloped or perhaps it's not that beneficial. Just because you think your idea is awesome, unfortunately, that doesn't mean that its marketable. There is definitely a method to objectively validate your vision and idea. There are many books and articles written on how to test your prototype thoroughly before launching a full-blown product.

5. *Be professional—act like a big company*

   Even if it's just you! It's crucial to project the appropriate image. Like you have it all together (i.e., your website, fulfillment, interaction with customers follow through, etc.). In this find-everything-on-the-Internet-era there are inexpensive freelancers for programming, manufacturing and personal assistants to help you manage and grow effectively. You can use an array of outside services from the Internet so you don't have to do it all yourself and you can utilize your limited resources to grow the business.

6. *Do it by the book—keep it legal*

   Before pursuing your passion, look through your company's contracts and non-disclosure agreement to see their policies. Ensure that what you are working on is totally unrelated to your company's business model. Also, work on your *own* equipment and on your *own* time, away from the office. To be 100% sure that your idea is not in direct conflict with your company's intellectual property, you may want to consult with an attorney.

7. *Devote your resources wisely (include time to network and any extra cash on hand to invest in your business)*

   As noted in the thirteen tips above it takes a herculean effort to network. Whether you're trying to climb the ladder in the corporate world or starting your own business, it's crucial you take the time to network. Also, invest wisely: i.e., a website, social media presence (Facebook and Twitter). Use some funds on Google AdWords to start building an email list. Don't waste your hard-earned money on office space or furniture. Work from home.

8. *Stop thinking about investors (initially)*

   If you are selling a service, there is no need for investors at this time. If you are designing a product for (hopefully) mass production, I know the I (investor) word pops up in your mind constantly. Who wouldn't want a couple of million dollars to quit their current job and hire some help to accelerate their product and business? However, it takes time, a long time to first design a pitch for investors, find investors, build a prototype, do marketing research, etc. Invest your time into moving your business forward rather than worrying about investors. The more mature your business is the more attractive it will look to investors in the future.

9. *You'll know when it's time to quit that day job*
Once you have a product or service that people want and you have paying customers, established the foundation (infrastructure and operations) for continuous business growth, a good marketing and sales system to generate leads and be able to close them—congratulations. Even if your income doesn't match your 9 to 5 job yet but, the business is ready and the customers want what you have, it's time to quit.

Conclusion—It's Your Livelihood—Make it Worthwhile

In this chapter the main theme is making the most out of your profession ASAP—your livelihood depends on success in your career and/or business. I discuss how Discipline and EQ play a major role facilitating your growth and getting you to that coveted success plateau. Follow my thirteen tips and make the most out of your career.

If you wanted to finally start that business you've been dreaming about for years—transitioning it to reality takes hard work, dedication and discipline! I have coached dozens of entrepreneurs with awesome ideas, however because they lack any sort of discipline, their ideas never see the light of day. Follow my nine tips on how to build a start-up business while working a 9 to 5 job.

In the next chapter my co-author A'ishah does a brilliant job communicating the importance of managing relationships. The bottom line is that it takes hard work, compromise and a lot of *discipline* to maintain a happy household.

Chapter 8

Manage Your Relationships

Self-respect is the key to respect, never lose your respect.

You can't earn your spouse's respect until you respect yourself. What does this imply? Essentially, to be able to build a great partnership, each of you must make an effort to develop your own weaknesses. Building and maintaining a solid relationship requires truly believing that excelling in self-discipline is the key to a successful "us," where you're not only working on your goals but also your goals as a couple.

It's so easy to get caught up with life's demands, we often get too comfortable and take our relationships for granted. For better or for worse, our partner will always be there, right? There will always be more activities on your plate than hours in a day to complete them—something has to give. Unfortunately, it's the areas we take for granted that are the first to give. Therefore, if you're in a relationship it's important you proactively manage it before it "gives."

In this chapter we cover the following topics to help guide you through key steps in an effort to fertilize and replenish any relationship:

- Why discipline in marriage
- A one-man show
- Motivation
- A subconscious desire to improve
- Realizing the ideal spouse, may not be so ideal
- Tackle it all at once
- Acquiring buy-in from your spouse
- Is marriage a compromise
- Time to accept and make a list
- Roles and responsibilities
- Ego and humility
- What does gender have to do with it
- Empathy
- Conflict management
- What does a great relationship look like

Adding the above to your tool belt will put you one big step ahead of the game. As the saying goes, "Happy spouse, happy house." Beginning each day with a content heart at home, will carry over into all aspects of your life making tackling life's difficulties just a bit easier.

Why Discipline in Marriage

What does your own self-discipline have to do with your marital relationship? Isn't being disciplined all about *you, your* goals, *your* time management practices, *your* priorities? Often individuals reach out for help with the following displaced mantra, "I am but one person, I must better myself to improve the marriage and all will fall into place." I know, because I too believed in this fast-paced, action-driven "I" based philosophy. With a history of independent accomplishments, many strongly believe that if they better themselves their marriage will automatically improve, as though with a wave of a wand all will be fixed. Unfortunately, this is wrong. While all it takes is one person to light the flame of change, it requires partnering with your spouse to sustain and uphold it.

This brings us to the question, what does it mean to incorporate discipline into a marriage? And why is it important for both partners to value discipline? Compared to just a decade ago, our lives have become *fast*, to say the least, and with this increase in speed we are seeing our modern technologically driven lives *demand* an increase in discipline to simply "keep up." Yet, we are regressing backwards toward a state of "checking out." Therefore, it is of no surprise that without the discipline needed we are seeing an increase in marital strife. With a sense of overwhelm, couples come home despondent, exhausted, and fatigued. Not the optimal ingredients needed for a healthy balanced marriage. Through counseling hundreds of singles and couples, Mr. Kern has seen firsthand the need for discipline to improve not only our individual lives but also our marriages.

After all, marriage is truly a partnership: between two individuals, two families, and two careers. You may be wondering what role a person's parental family and career play. Understanding these foundational aspects of life are crucial to understanding yourself, which in turn enables us to make better decisions for ourselves and our marriages. Our upbringing, defined by our families, are but who we are; whether positive or negative. They shape and define us for better or for worse. In addition, our careers are a major rate-limiting or rate-nourishing aspect of our lives. Our jobs dictate our daily schedules and hence our priorities; whether we can fit everything we "want" to do into a day, while bringing home a paycheck to afford it, essentially defines our roles, responsibilities, and priorities. Therefore, taking the time to understand these aspects of ourselves is important to help merge the lives of two different individuals in a relationship.

In essence, if what you strive for is discipline in your daily marital life, then look to your significant other. Was he or she raised with discipline? What habits and practices are deeply rooted in him/her? Does his/her work schedule prohibit or encourage discipline? And the most important question of all, is your partner "wanting" to change as much as you, for without him/her at your side, this will be an uphill battle to say the least. The realization of this early on, along with the buy-in from your partner, will save you much grief, frustration, and time.

A One-Man Show

The following case study reveals the relevance and impact of self-discipline on a relationship that came through with flying colors as BOTH partners worked through Mr. Kern's couple's coaching.

> *Highly successful, ambitious, accomplished, every goal achieved to the highest level, accolades abound. This was the wife, a Non-Stop One-Man Show. She managed her life, her career, her education, and her family. What more could anyone want, right? She accomplished all of her goals, so she assumed she could achieve*

anything she wanted. Staying up late, sacrificing social events, eating unhealthily, exercising rarely, cramming last minute, ALL were major undisciplined habits she used to accomplish her goals. Throw marriage into the mix of it and she went from a one-man show to a partnership. After all, she asked him all the right questions before getting married, there should have been no problems, right? Are you clean and organized? Check. Are you healthy? Check. Are you religious? Check. Are you motivated? Check. The big mistake was that his definition of "yes" did not match hers. Rather than asking closed-ended questions, she should have asked open ended questions to understand his viewpoint...and then they were married. For Better or For Worse. She believed they were a perfect match made in heaven, with all the same values, goals, and habits...they were both in for a surprise!

Only a year or so into the marriage, the wife reverted to her one-man show habits. She believed that by working on her self-discipline she could then essentially MAKE her partner adopt the same habits. However, as she struggled to undo decades of undisciplined habits and force these onto her partner, she realized her husband was slowing her down and this led to significant marital strife. The sad part was, that was not his intention nor was it hers. Neither of them wanted this struggle and essentially desired similar goals, but they were both too independent-minded to understand it.

This couple eventually did learn that to achieve self-discipline in their lives, their marriage, and their future, both partners needed to see eye-to-eye while making discipline a priority. Now that did not require both persons to have the same definition of discipline, but it did mean both persons needed to be on the same page to be able to make decisions together. For a partnership to work, it takes two to tango. Once both partners in this relationship learned the difference between a marriage that simply coexists versus a partnership aimed at creating something better, they were on the path to a better future.

Motivation

We ALL have struggles, no one is excluded. I grew up in a household in love with Bollywood movies. To those unfamiliar with this genre of fiction, it requires a suspension of all reality. Familiar with Disney fairy tales, well Bollywood takes the prince woos princess to a whole new level. With the hero jumping from ten story buildings, motorcycles leaping across mountainous heights, and a playboy hero falling head over heels over the simpleton girl…really? And yet millions believe it all—love was enough to make it all work magically. But does the social media/Hollywood/Bollywood fantasy exist? The next snapchat or Facebook picture your friend posts, stop and ask yourself, "what is the background story to this?"

Marriage is a test, go digging around in the scriptures of any religion and you'll find marriage defined as a challenge that requires work, perseverance, and faith built on basic principles of truth, loyalty and respect. Such deep words, ouch. Nothing like the fairy tales. The first step to seeing eye-to eye with your spouse is differentiating the fantasy from the reality. The fantasy depicted on social media and in the movies is only a snapshot of reality and the hard work pays off when you get these "moments" of fantasy. But the reality is, it will require hard work on a constant basis.

So, where does one start? Especially when you already feel overwhelmed and lost from your own lack of self-discipline and now you have the added task of a partner with whom you are not seeing eye-to eye. Start by travelling back in time, think back to why you married this person and if needed dig deep to see the positives. Remembering why you felt this marriage was good for you will provide the motivation needed to persevere through the hard work required to fix your relationship.

A Subconscious Desire to Improve

As the pursuit to marital bliss continues, and trust me it will be a relentless pursuit until the end, the question worth answering FIRST is, "Why did I marry my spouse?" Whether we realize it or not, we select our partners to fill and/or cure our inadequacies.... hence opposites commonly attract as Paula Abdul adequately stated. But to the contrary of her lyrics, it's not a chemical attraction, it's purposeful and intentional. Our minds know what they're doing. It's what I refer to as, "a subconscious desire to improve."

We look for someone who is the opposite of us, everything we want to be but are not. Two very different personalities locked inside a single home. The problem is, in this desperate effort to escape from our own reality we often swing too far to the other end of the pendulum without even realizing it, and the marriage without work continues to swing back and forth between the two polar extremes. Once the inertia of marriage is set in motion it becomes VERY difficult to break this cycle. Without work this pendulum will continue to swing back and forth, creating havoc, desperation and chaos in a relationship requiring tranquility to face life's constant challenges. As Newton's law of motion describes, "an object at rest will remain at rest and an object in motion will stay in motion unless it is acted on by an unbalanced force." Finding the unbalanced force to create change, now that is the tricky part that leads to many broken relationships.

Referring back to the "one-man show" case study mentioned earlier. In the beginning of this relationship, the wife often asked herself, "Did I make a mistake marrying my spouse?" The negativity of this question itself portrays the self-loathing, perfectionistic, super-controlling inadequacies within that led her to her husband, who was the most carefree, *laissez-faire* person in existence…SEE the polar opposites! She was so enamored by his free-spirit, she failed to see his supreme laziness. A husband content with the bare minimum. She loved his genius mind but loathed his lack of desire to rise and create change. In the beginning she blamed herself for selecting the wrong spouse, but in reality, he was EXACTLY what she needed.

One might even say she could clearly see the fire yet walked straight into it. Comments from friends & family emphasizing laziness, anger, a predisposition to arguing were common, but she chose to ignore these red flags. On the contrary, he was her prince in shining armor, he swept her off her feet and imbued in her a sense of calm she had never felt before. A "legal" euphoric high that she most desperately wanted in life. How was she to know this was only the calm before the storm.

Looking at such relationships from the outside, one wonders, was it self-sabotage or self-improvement the wife in this case study was looking for. In selecting her partner did she sabotage herself, a punishment of some sorts for the many flaws she saw in herself and wanted to escape from. Or was it her struggle to improve herself, a betterment project. Either way, it was her conscious decision based on subconscious motives. Whether self-sabotage or self-improvement, we often enter a relationship to be surprised. Your partner ends up being not what you expected BUT rather the opposite; a reflection of your best AND worst nightmares. Scary thought, yet we do it to ourselves and we are not alone.

Realizing the Ideal Spouse, May Not be so Ideal

Before I met my husband, I listed all the top qualities I felt I needed in a spouse to a girlfriend of mine and asked, "Why can't I find a guy like that?" Her response blew me away to a *new* level of understanding myself. She answered, *"Because then you would not be so perfect anymore."* The "ideal" spouse would have highlighted everything I was not and quite frankly he deserved someone a bit more on his plane. The responsibility cannot lay solely on one person, he/she will eventually become resentful. For a relationship to work, both partners must serve as a mirror for each other—the perfectly unperfect couple.

In fact, we are inherently hardwired to select the perfectly imperfect partner. Think about it. As often is the case, each of us has likely met and rejected that "ideal" guy. You know the one: extremely disciplined with morning and evening routines, intelligent, adored you, willing to change and improve, a go-getter and highly motivated…BUT this person just did not appeal to you. There must be a reason our minds work this way. David Peck attempts to answer this by defining four important ingredients needed for people to change: capability, awareness, fire (strong desire to change), and timing. Although great, the "ideal" suitor often does not invoke any of these four ingredients leading to the lack of chemical attraction. After all, who doesn't crave a relationship with "fire"!

Interestingly enough, a speaker at a recent wedding I attended hit the nail on the head when he said, "Marriage is when your partner brings out the better in you." By being the strong protagonist in your life your partner will push you to dive deep and see your reflection in the mirror for the first time. Then out of desperation—to say the least—force you to improve. This desperation is often the needed 'fire" to fuel your change. Your life may have been quite emptily perfect prior to this protagonist, requiring this "fire" to break you and force the rebuilding phase. As Malcolm Gladwell states, we each have our own tipping point that must be reached for major change to come about. *Everything* happens for a reason; it is purposeful. Your spouse may not be who you thought he was, rather he is better because he is exactly what you need!

Tackle it All at Once

You married your protagonist to change, now what? Self-sabotage or self-improvement, it no longer matters. Regardless of the subconscious motive behind the selection of your spouse, the more difficult steps lay ahead. As you struggle to internalize the benefits, remind yourself it will take time and effort to create change.

For starters, stop solely pointing out your partner's weaknesses. Most counselors would say, focus on your partner's strengths. This is where I differ. When you are in the midst of marital strife it is difficult to do this while ignoring the overwhelming weight of your partner's weaknesses. When the scale has tipped and all you can see are the negatives far outweighing the positives, how does a person focus solely on their partner's strengths? The answer is not simple. It is a multi-step process that cannot occur in sequential order, but rather must be tackled ALL at once:

1. *Develop your own weaknesses, while focusing on your partner's strengths.*

   In marriage our vision often becomes clouded by all the baggage that has accumulated, making it difficult to see your partner's strengths. Remind yourself that you are not perfect and have your own set of issues to work on, this will help clear your field of vision and enable you to focus on why you married that person. After all, in the "one-man show" case study, her husband was the only person who provided her high-anxiety, perfectionistic personality a sense of calm; a major strength that can be invaluable in the face of life's many challenges.

2. *You must learn to respect and see your OWN strengths; stop being your own worst critic!*

   Relationships are hard and if you're reading this book, you are a unique individual with a personal strength to be explored. Self-discipline, learning who you are, and achieving our best self—that is the goal. After all, until we love ourselves, how can we love another. Recall the quote mentioned at the beginning of this chapter, it comes from my father who would often say, "Self-respect is the key to respect, so never lose yourself in the process."

3. *As hard as it might seem, you MUST stop pointing out your partner's flaws.*

   Who wants to hear constant nagging and criticism? The partner who nags likely grew up with an external voice of constant critique, so this person will need to learn to fight the urge to continue this soul crushing habit. If you're seeking perfection from your partner—as Mr. Kern would say: *"Really?"*

4. *Focus on "understanding" the beauty in your partner's weaknesses.*

   Most of us view our weaknesses as negative qualities that must be changed or removed. The truth is, these weaknesses are likely hardwired into our existence and their removal is highly unlikely. Instead, view your so-called weaknesses through a positive lens as potential strengths. Perhaps the power above, if you believe in one, gave you these weaknesses not only as a struggle but also a strength, which once understood could be used for positive change. For example, my entire life I had been criticized for being too detailed, but once I learned to balance this quality it became a strength. To do so required a re-training of my mind. I had to learn that some things were worth the time needed to scrutinize every detail while others were not; it was not an all or none way of living. *Realizing the shelves in the shoe closet did not NEED to be perfect the time was better spent reviewing the details of the building structure and tilework (items not hidden away inside a closet and covered by dirty shoes!).* However, habits die hard, and it still requires a constant effort on my part to maintain this balance.

I cannot emphasize enough the importance of tackling all four of these steps simultaneously. Attempting to do any one of these steps sequentially may have deleterious effects. For instance, if a person were to focus on the first step listed alone, that person may become submissive due to feelings of guilt and inferiority caused by a focus on their weaknesses and their partner's strengths. However, if the other three elements are emphasized simultaneously, it creates a balance of sorts. All couples, whether they realize it or not, struggle for power; harmony comes with balance.

Acquiring Buy-in From Your Spouse

Using the approach presented in this chapter and book will help you re-ignite the positive memory that led you to marrying your spouse while simultaneously working on your own self-discipline. However, without your spouse's cooperation and buy-in, improving the marriage alone will be an uphill battle. Regardless of how hard you try it will be a slippery slope downward without your partner's participation. To have self-discipline at home, your partner must be on board to create the team-based approach needed for a successful enterprise.

So how do you acquire buy-in from your spouse? Often in a relationship, one person will be in a different place in their quest for personal development, making gaining the reluctant partner's buy-in tricky. After all, if he/she believes they are fine, why would he/she want to put in the enormous amount of work required to create change. Especially if the partner is controlled by ego, obtaining buy-in will be even more difficult. The answer to this dilemma is almost always: humility, love and kindness. Always ask nicely and at first be ready to hear your partner say "no."

Returning back to our "one-man show" case study, the husband was initially quite irritable and upset at the thought of needing a coach. Understandably so, being a reputable lawyer, he felt he didn't need anyone's help to accomplish anything. Therefore, when first asked to work with his wife and Mr. Kern as a coach, his response was, "I can do it myself." With kindness the wife accepted and allowed her husband to try. After multiple failed attempts the husband finally beseeched a bit of control and agreed to participate. Now keep in mind, although the husband verbally said he was on board, these were just words and again it took time until he truly saw the value of the coaching sessions. This made things very frustrating for the wife, as she wanted change and wanted it now. However, each of us must meet the key ingredients for change on their own terms (capability, awareness, fire, and timing), it cannot be forced. With patience and perseverance, many months later her husband finally changed his attitude and said, "I can live up to my potential please give me time, I'm trying."

Keep in mind, change can not only bring two persons together, but it can also pull two persons apart. Neither path being wrong. For fear of the possible negative outcome, often couples do not push themselves to face this fork in the road. However, once you sense you are at this junction, it will be necessary to face the truth with no regrets. Ask yourselves, are we in the same place at this moment in our life and do we both want the same future? The hope is for the answer to be a mutual reconcilable one with a common goal to strive for.

Is Marriage a Compromise

Always remember, for *any* relationship to be healthy and balanced it must start with unconditional love, a combination of what I call the holy words: patience, self-control, honesty, and humility...words that imbibe all that is good and pure and admirable. Unconditional love with gratitude for what you have will give you a clearer focus on the positives in your life and hence the strength to deal with the negatives. Kindness and gratitude were my two selected "mantra" words to remind me of this key principle. Select yours, take a deep breath, and let's begin…oh yes, we are just beginning!

Once both partners are working together toward self-discipline individually and also within their marriage, what's next? Now this is where it gets tricky. I've heard many counselors advise their clients that marriage is a compromise. I'm not so sure on this. Compromise is defined as, "an agreement or settlement of a dispute that is reached by each side making concessions" or "the acceptance of standards that are lower than is desirable." How can such negative connotations make for a good relationship? Why should anyone accept standards lower than desirable?

Before answering these questions, let's look at the difference between three very similar words: "adept," "adopt," and "adapt." As I mentioned earlier, relationships are often a struggle for power, making understanding these three words helpful as you take on a new approach to tackling this struggle. (http://www.learnersdictionary.com/qa/adept-adapt-or-adopt). Adept is an adjective and the other two words are verbs. The definition of all three words is different:

- Adept means 'good at doing something difficult.'
- Adopt usually means 'to take something legally as your own.'
- Adapt means 'to change for a new situation or purpose.'

Now each partner comes into the relationship feeling **adept** or good at what they do, so he/she will naturally assume it is not them but rather the partner that must change to improve the marriage. However, if you feel this way, remind yourself that you married your spouse for a reason, because he/she is good at certain things. Taking the time to understand and highlight these positive characteristics will help you respect your spouse, making it easier to acknowledge what strengths each of you brings to the table.

Next, we come to the word **adopt.** In a relationship, adopting will not serve you well either. Think about it, would you want to take on what your spouse does or says and assume it to be your own way of thinking, behaving and being? I wouldn't, I am after all an independent individual with my own set of strengths. Rather a marriage should help each individual grow for the better, not lose sight of who they are by adopting their spouse's traits.

This leaves us with my favorite word when it comes to marriage: **adapt.** This word inherently includes change, BUT more importantly it is change without losing sight of who you are. You still maintain your "adept" skills and "adopt" the positive attributes of your spouse, but rather than completely changing yourself you "adapt" to the relationship. By working with your spouse, you come up with new skills that are a combination of the two of you. Something you alone would not have achieved. Rather than viewing marriage as two persons compromising, learn to look at it as creating a *new* path unique to the two of you.

Time to Accept and Make a List

Now having understood the difference between adept, adopt, and adapt, it is time to *accept*. While you both struggle to create this "new path" in your marriage, the truth of the matter is, your spouse will not be able to adapt *all* the traits you deem undesirable. Leaving you with an important question to answer, "Who I thought you were, and who you truly are, is the difference acceptable?" Answering this question will force you to make a conscious decision (no more subconscious desires clouding your judgement) of whether you want to move forward in this relationship or not.

This is where you must dig deep, separate yourself from the Bollywood/social media fallacies, and truly try and understand yourself and your values. At no point should anyone compromise their moral, religious, or personal scruples. In fact, make a list and show it to your partner. Explain to him or her that these are the top five to ten items that define your happiness and be open with him; explain why these top items are so important to you. Often when our spouses understand the reasoning behind our requests, they are more apt to listen. Also, don't forget to ask your partner to make a similar list.

Going back to the "one-man show" case study, the wife came up with a list of seven items and she related the importance of all seven items to raising a child. She explained to her husband that she saw these seven items as weaknesses in both herself and him, and she tied the importance of these items back to religion and self-discipline. She asked her husband, "If we do not change these items in ourselves then how can we expect anything different from our kids?" The husband responded by saying he would "try" with no defensive argument back! Definitely a win response.

After this open discussion, come up with a final couple's list that identifies what can and cannot be changed or will require more time. Although this is a final list for now, always remember this is a dynamic process, which means this so-called "final" list will be edited along the way. A trait your spouse feels he can change today, he may realize over time change in this area is not possible, or vice versa. The key will be to not expect overnight change and to trust that time will reveal to you what is or isn't a realistic expectation. In fact, as certain traits improve, you yourself may not deem other items as highly as you did before. When this happens, be careful not to let ego take over, as it is okay to admit to your spouse that what was initially important to you is now irrelevant.

The path will be a constant test of patience, stressing the importance of empathy along the way. Often you will have to swallow certain things because your spouse is not fully developed yet—bite your tongue! When things get difficult, remind yourself that some things cannot be changed. Rather than stressing out, be patient, time will reveal a happy median that will work for the both of you.

As you continually define and redefine your top priority items for change in your partner, I cannot emphasize how much you will also learn about yourself in the process. An example from a couples' case study exemplifies this. When the couple first got married, the wife expected her husband to keep his closet perfectly aligned with *all* his shelf items properly folded in clean straight lines. But as time went on, the wife realized no one would be able to fold and maintain a pile of clothes the same way she did. In fact, she learned through her own self-discovery process that baskets are great! Rather than folding everything, like underwear, throw them in a basket by category, it's still organized and no minutes will be lost folding. When she passed this suggestion on to her husband, it was a win-win discussion. If her husband was trying his best and his closet no longer looked like a tsunami had crushed through it, she was ready to *accept* his effort. She realized it was more important to focus on growing as individuals and as a couple.

On a more practical note, how do you keep track of your final list to know how your spouse is doing? I suggest making an excel chart and listing your agreed upon traits relative to the date. Then each of you can keep a daily record if the goal was achieved, not achieved, or missed for a valid reason. Setup weekly discussions with your partner to see how things are going, discuss what you are willing to accept and decide if you need to redefine anything. A word of advice, always look at the negatives relative to the positives and see if the pros outweigh the cons, after all no one is perfect. Remember you married that person for a reason.

Roles and Responsibilities

Understanding roles and responsibilities can also help you cut down the nonsense and focus on the bigger things. Roles and responsibilities are unique to each couple and must be identified relative to an individual's strengths/weaknesses *and* time limitations. For instance, although my husband is much more knowledgeable and efficient at dealing with house contractors or car repairs than I am, this responsibility mostly falls on me since I work part-time. He is the primary bread-winner of the house, I cannot expect him to take time off and lose his salary to deal with a contractor. As much as I struggle with these tasks, I must learn to *adapt* and deal with these items. Another example is cooking, considering I am home most days of the week I become the primary cook for the household and there is absolutely nothing sexist about it. As long as each spouse continues to show appreciation to the other, in the end it makes the effort feel worthwhile. A simple smile and thank you goes a long way!

Once you can identify and truly understand not only your spouse's strengths & weaknesses but also your own, respect will follow. In fact, knowing each other's roles and responsibilities allows one to then go the extra mile. I am also not a morning person, so in the beginning of our marriage I never even fathomed the need to get up early and help ensure my husband ate something in the morning. But once we better delineated our roles and responsibilities, and as an extension I developed a respect for my husband providing financially for our family, I naturally went the extra mile *(without even thinking)* and woke up early to warm him some breakfast. The first time I did this he thanked me and said, "I had been leaving for work hungry, thank you, this helps a lot." Change is a two-way streak, but there is nothing wrong in taking the first step; control your ego and happily take the first step.

Ego and Humility

Unfortunately, taking the first step or learning to *adapt* to your spouse is often taken in our fast-paced modern times as a sign of weakness or submissiveness. "I will not let my marriage change who I am!" is a common phrase. To be bluntly honest, this sort of mentality will only guarantee you failure. Rather, we need a change in the way we think—yes, we should not lose the good things about ourselves *but* we need to be ready to embrace change as a blending of personalities and cultures to create something *new* and better—an Adaptation.

In fact, there are three key viewpoints we need to understand to help us embrace this change in our life. First, as I just mentioned, it starts with a change in the way we think. Simply acknowledging that you are open to change will make the path easier. Second, we need to work to understand our ego to be able to suppress it. Trust me, ego in a marriage is never helpful! Let go of your Ego, be humble and remember couples are partners on the same team. Third, although I strongly believe men and women are created equal, I have learned over time that each gender is genetically encoded UN-equal. We've heard the saying, men are from Mars and women are from Venus, right? Well, it's very true! We are created equal, but with different strengths and weaknesses making us uniquely different. In fact, understanding this gender difference is pivotal in being able to let go of one's ego. The mistake comes when people translate these differences into a competition to judge who is better. The earlier in the relationship each spouse understands and *accepts* these three points of view, the easier it will be.

To exemplify the third viewpoint just mentioned, an important gender difference worth acknowledging is the tendency for men's ego to make them defensive while women tend to be forgiving. Characteristics genetically encoded in each gender to maintain a home. Think about it, men need to be defensive to protect their family from outside forces. While women need to be forgiving to go through childbirth and raise children. The key is for these traits not to be taken advantage of. Men please remember, humility is not a sign of weakness. Genuinely saying you're sorry with an effort to improve will only elevate you in the eyes of your spouse. When it comes to your wife, stop the excuses and defensiveness, the only purpose they serve is to fuel the fire of unreconcilable arguments. Instead take ownership for your mistakes and embrace humility, it will help you bite your tongue when appropriate. When you've made a mistake, trust me, women are quicker to forgive when they are not fed a bunch of excuses. In fact, how many of us have heard the wedding speech, you know the one where the best man jokes, "Happy wife equals happy life." When the macho husband learns proving himself is not necessary, humility (with a dash of subservience) follows giving way for a woman's naturally forgiving side to take over.

What Does Gender Have to Do with it?

Another important gender difference highlights emotions: a man's lack of ability to share compared to a woman who is genetically encoded to be emotionally expressive, again both desirable traits for maintaining a household. The key is to understand how to strike a working balance between the two. Here the ominous duty falls heavily on the wife. How many times have I heard a woman say, "I can tell he is in pain, he even complained about it, but the next moment he is out mowing the lawn?" Back off women! All you can do is use your empathy and emotions to pick up on the pain and offer your husband your assistance, then wait patiently until they are ready for help. While I ask men to subdue their egos, this is not the job of the wife. A woman attacking a man's ego is one of the biggest fundamental mistakes that can be made. Telling him he is too weak to mow the lawn is the last thing he wants to hear, regardless of the reason. Give your husband some space and do not push him too hard.

Along the same lines is the example of the husband who is in pain and extremely tired from working the graveyard shift yet doesn't say a word of complaint. The wife consumed with her own workload continues to push the husband with daily house tasks. Until one day the husband explodes and both partners are confused as to what happened. Hoping your husband will simply "open up" may not be a realistic expectation. Rather use your innate emotional skills to note a change in his mood or behavior and be empathetic to his limitations, whether physical or social (i.e., work schedules). One person in any relationship will always be more disciplined or have more time, accepting this will foster empathy and make being mindful of your partner's needs easier. Once we are more empathetic, the expectations become more natural and comfortable.

Another invaluable piece of advice for men: MARK YOUR CALENDARS! Women as I mentioned are created to be emotional and this is especially true during their monthly menstrual cycles (it's in their genes and is necessary for motherhood). Men please understand, it is *normal* for women to be emotional and confusing during this time. Who would enjoy feeling bloated, gaining extra pounds of water, burning hot from the inside, back pain, leg pain, headaches and irritability? The sooner men learn how to respond to their wives' changes the more peaceful life will be. Fortunately, the cycle repeats in a cyclical and, lucky for men, predictable manner. Allowing men to easily mark two important weeks on their calendar: The PMS week (generally the seven days leading up to the start of the menstrual week) and the week of the actual menses. This will keep you on your toes, encouraging you to be more sensitive and reminding you to bite your tongue! On the flipside, advice to the women: please do not try to deny this truth. Often women believe they are the exception to the rule and proclaim they are not as bad as "other" women. This is false as ALL women go through this to varying degrees and it is never easy for the male gender. In fact, I encourage women to mark their calendars as well to help identify a change in their mood so they too can be more vigilant. Once both partners understand this concept, empathy naturally follows.

Empathy

Now, the combination of letting go of one's ego, expressing or lack of expressing one's emotions, identifying biological patterns, and understanding roles and responsibilities, all helps free your mind from the constant fight for control and blame in a relationship. "Why should I do that? Why can't he help with this? Just because

I'm a woman I have to cook?" Your mind suddenly becomes free to simply act. With all this freed up mental RAM, a person naturally becomes more aware of their spouse's emotional well-being, which indelibly creates empathy. You will begin to respect your partner more as you appreciate the things, he/she is doing for the family. As I have already mentioned multiple times in this chapter, empathy will be KEY to getting you through this, it all works full circle.

In fact, empathic conversations need to be practiced. The honeymoon phase is over! You are two unique individuals who think in different ways, which naturally requires work and practice to keep any relationship going. Empathic conversations can be practiced through "role playing" exercises. Trade places with your spouse and first respond with what he/she actually said, then rather than criticizing their response simply state what you would have preferred to hear and how it would have been more helpful to you. For example, one day I was venting to my husband my frustration with a friend who had copied my entire project theme and then took this a step further by posting a LOOONG essay online about the creativity and forethought it required. It was a flagrant copy of my hard work, not that I wanted any credit, but to act as though they had come up with everything on their own was annoying to say the least. My husband's response was, "Why are you making a big deal out of nothing, who cares." When I explained to him that all he needed to say was, "Honey, I can see how this is upsetting; they used your ideas and took credit for them. I am here to comfort and listen to you, but try to remember we are happy now and that is what is more important." A big hug would have been the cherry on top. Often all women need is for men to show that they understand their feelings, it's as simple as that...really, it is!

Conflict Management

While I cannot guarantee the techniques discussed thus far will work for you, what I can guarantee is, "it is not *if* bad times will arise, it is *when* bad times will arise." Despite empathy, conflicts will inevitably arise making it important to learn some conflict management techniques to use in the "heat" of the moment. As mentioned earlier, a simple tip is to mark your calendars to anticipate the arrival of the infamous menstrual cycle. Be empathetic and learn how to respond to your partner during this time. You can even practice these conversations beforehand or at the least bite your tongue.

Another technique is the interjection of humor during a highly emotional conversation. One person will always be more upset than the other, making it the responsibility of the relatively calmer partner to attempt this strategy. In fact, you can both agree on a "trigger" word beforehand, something that will naturally remind you of a funny moment. Think of a time you both laughed out loud or an experience that was absurdly funny. Once you both agree on this event/moment, select a key word to remind you of this experience. By mentioning this word during a heated conversation, it will trigger happy thoughts and quickly bring them to the surface. Remember, when emotions rise logical thinking naturally drops. By using this trigger word to bring a smile to your faces, you are putting out the fire just enough to regain the balance between emotion and logical thinking.

If all else fails, stay quiet. How many of you are married to a defensive hothead? The hothead person in the relationship is often the biggest baby, but with understanding and love even the hottest of hotheads can be tamed. The day their partner realizes the anger is simply a childlike tantrum, he/she learns to react the way one would to a toddler throwing a fit. Stay calm and quiet, do not respond, and walk away. Usually the hothead will calm him/herself down and return with everything worked out. Easier said than done though, learning to stay quiet in the moment and walking away is the ultimate test of patience.

What Does a Great Relationship Look Like?

A great relationship is one in which two people work together toward a common goal. It is not abusive in any manner. It is communicating and coming to a common understanding; there are no winners because you worked together. Below are twenty tips taught by Mr. Kern on how to build and maintain a "great" relationship.

Twenty Tips on How to Build and Maintain a Great Relationship

1. *Trust is the foundation for a strong relationship*
   Think about all the people you know that question their partners about every little detail of the day. Trust is vital for any relationship to become strong and everlasting.

2. *Honesty IS the best policy*
   Even white lies eventually turn into big lies that forever need to be covered up. Lies are like a poisonous gas that will silently kill any relationship. Never lie!

3. *Spend quality time together*
   Small acts can go a long way. Use dinner time to have meaningful discussions with the TV and both phones turned off. Afterwards, take a nightly walk together then relax and watch something on Netflix. Also, don't forget to schedule that occasional date night.

4. *Continue to be best friends*
   You started out as friends and you should continue to cultivate your friendship. Take the time to discuss the good and the bad that each day brings your way. The more you communicate, the closer friends you become.

5. *Communication is crucial*
   Communication is a vital success factor in any relationship. How else are you supposed to know what your partner is thinking or what is going on in their lives? Couples in successful relationships consistently express their love for each other, complement one another frequently, and never avoid discussing difficult issues.

6. *It takes work—set goals*
   Establish personal and companionship goals. Whether it's financial or a special romantic vacation—see those goals through to fruition and then celebrate together. Achieving a couple's goal is a key success factor and an excellent bonding experience.

7. *It takes two to Tango*
   Look for common ground during arguments. It doesn't matter who is to blame. You have too many other things to worry about. Not every couple is going to agree on everything.

8. *Never go to sleep during a heated argument*
   Make every possible effort to resolve the disagreement before going to sleep or at the very least, never go to bed angry with each other.

9. *Don't cause a disturbance*

    Yelling, throwing, hitting objects or storming out of a room and slamming a door will only exacerbate a negative situation. Don't make a scene. Find ways to release tension and calm down (i.e., exercise, walk around the block or simply let some time elapse) then gently discuss the issue.

10. *Don't dwell on negative scenarios from the past*

    Raising issues from the past will only cause friction and make the current situation worse. Don't go there. You don't need to rehash the past, deal with the present.

11. *Choose your words carefully—Respect your partner at all times*

    Just like choosing words carefully in the workplace there is no difference here—be politically astute! Don't mock or belittle. Be kind, soft-spoken, well-mannered, don't talk negatively to friends and family about your relationship and never threaten to leave. Treat your partner as you wish to be treated.

12. *Forgiveness is essential*

    Forgive your partner's harsh or offensive words every now and then. As long as this does not happen daily or even weekly, find it in your heart to forgive your partner.

13. *Really listen to your partner*

    Don't interrupt, even if it's a heated discussion. Give your partner your full attention and really try to understand your partner's perspective. There is nothing more annoying than talking to someone's back.

14. *Don't just blurt out a problem—provide a solution first*

   For example, don't just blame your partner for not cooking. Rather, schedule a time for the both of you to cook together.

15. *Manage yourself, not your partner*

   Worry about yourself and be the best you can be. The more efficient you become, the more productive you will be, leaving you with more time for one another.

16. *Sex...*

   It's important to maintain your sex life and keep it interesting, spontaneous and unpredictable. Don't just do it for the sake of doing it.

17. *Display appreciation—honor your partner with love every day*

   It does not take much effort—do things you know your partner enjoys. Whether it's romantic words, flowers, love notes, cards, quality time, acts of kindness, or physical touch, "show" your special someone you love them.

18. *Don't compare your life to others*

   We tend to compare our relationships to those of others. This is made easier than ever with social media. The grass isn't always greener on the other side. Focus on your relationship!

19. *Maintain your own identity*

   Everyone knows spending quality time together is important, but spending time apart is important too. Keep your own interests and continuously develop yourself.

20. *Bring your partner into your world*
Make every attempt to summarize your responsibilities/tasks to your partner. For example, if you're managing the finances for the household, always update your partner. Create a formal spreadsheet which you can review together at least monthly.

To reiterate a very important message: after you've established a strong relationship, always proactively manage it. Just because things are going well today doesn't mean they will remain that way. Things can change suddenly and could cost you dearly if you are not prepared.

Conclusion—The Beginning to Your Destiny

I hope I have not made this sound like a simple quick fix guide, because relationship management is not and will never be. It will take time and will be an ongoing struggle as you both go through different phases of your lives. While these techniques are not quick fixes they can be applied to life's changing challenges. Whether this advice works will truly depend on whether the two of you are compatible. However, if these techniques are not working for you, please do seek the counsel of an expert third party professional who can intervene. As eventually you will need to face the truth and answer the tough questions...but until then, let's think positively and move forward.

In the next chapter Mr. Kern discusses two of the most important facets to maintaining good health: exercising consistently and managing your meal intake. We all know that exercise and eating right are the key catalysts to maintaining a healthy lifestyle. He introduces his 10x10 tips to help you achieve your health goals.

—A'ishah Khan

Chapter 9

Govern Your Health

The better you manage your health the more productive you become. You may not be aware of this, but your body craves a strong health regimen and is energized by it. As a result, the more energetic you are the more you are able to accomplish. In addition to your energy level, your outlook on life, stress levels and clarity to strategize are all greatly improved. Improving your health can even help improve your mental health. I am not a physician, but I've worked with dozens of clients in my life who had severe depression and/or high anxiety; improving their health immensely helped ameliorate their symptoms!

Managing Your Health Must be a Daily Priority

In fact, being in good health is a prerequisite to building the best version of you. This means managing your health should be a daily priority, not something done occasionally. Your mind needs your body in perfect condition. By perfect I mean the best condition that you are able to achieve given your circumstances. Without your body in the best possible condition, you will be adding another obstacle to your road to success.

So how does one achieve a healthy regimen? Is this just another diet fad? From my experience and research, governing your health essentially includes two main components; managing your food intake and exercising consistently. In this chapter, I will highlight tips that I have developed over the years to help you optimize both of these areas. I call them my "10 x 10 tips" to a healthy way of living.

Exercise Consistently

What is exercise? Dictionary.com defines exercise as *bodily or mental exertion, especially for the sake of training or improvement of health.* The idea is to move. Any movement is better than no movement. Think of exercise as a stimulant to make you more productive. Even though you will come up with loads of excuses why you shouldn't exercise—you need to just do it! You will feel great the entire day! Below are my ten tips to help you exercise consistently.

Ten Tips to Help You Exercise Consistently

1. *Make exercise a daily habit*
   Please stop setting that silly goal of exercising only three days a week. We all know that three days will turn into two days and then one day and eventually another failed goal. This is common practice. Instead, begin with a mindset change to include exercise as part of your daily routine. Yes, I'm saying it needs to become a daily habit or you might as well go back to your old three-day a week (failed) program.

2. *Have a positive attitude*
   Be positive—you know the results of consistently exercising are second-to-none. Think of the results, not how tired you might be on any given day. If you take on the challenge of exercising every day along with a negative attitude, your new goal will never see the light of day.

3. *Exercise in the morning prior to work*
   The best way to remain consistent is to exercise each morning before going to work. The excuses are fewer in the morning since you have to get up early and go to work anyway. Whether you work from home or travel to an office, there are too many excuses why you shouldn't exercise after work, with the most common ones being: "I'm too tired, it's been a long day, I have too much work to do or I don't feel well."

4. *Discipline your evening*
   Follow a good PM routine that has you winding down and getting ready for bed at a decent hour in order to get ample sleep and feel well-rested in the morning. You will have a quality workout if you are well-rested.

5. *Establish doable targets*
   If you're someone who has difficulties achieving your exercise-related goals, be realistic and start out small. Perhaps walking around the block every day (assuming you live on a small block) and then after one week increasing your distance by walking around the same block two times.

6. *Make exercise fun*
   Exercise does not need to be misery inducing. Yet so many people look upon it as a necessary evil with nothing but

sweat and pain. If this is you, it's time to get creative. How can you make it fun? Do you like variety? Do you need a partner? Do you need support? Do you need incentives? Do you like to dance? Do you like being out in nature? Is it more fun when it's a group setting? Do you like to compete against yourself or others? Try out different exercise possibilities and find what's right for you. When exercise becomes fun, it becomes natural and that is the goal.

7. *You don't have to attend a gym*
   Our bodies need some form of exercise on a regular basis, but you don't have to go to the gym each day.

   a. Clean your house or apartment once a week at a fast pace
   b. Wash/wax your own car
   c. Take long brisk walks to the store, or around the block at work
   d. Take the stairs at work instead of the elevator

   You have many options—just do it!

8. *Establish phrases—play mind games*
   Train your mind to believe exercise is not a supplement; it's an integral part of your life. Use negative phrases or positive affirmations/techniques to train your mind (see Chapter One).
   Repeatedly tell yourself the following negative phrases:

   a. You're pathetic and you need to get your fat lazy butt out of bed earlier and go exercise.
   b. You look like crap—get off the couch and do something about it.

c. You can't walk down that beach with that big stomach. Go do something about that disgusting gut.

Utilize the following techniques for positive reactions:

a. Visualize yourself enjoying exercise, winning at it.
b. Think of an image that gets you excited about exercising.
c. Imagine being admired by your friends for how fit you are.
d. Give yourself a pep talk.
e. Hook up with someone, such as a trainer, a coach or a loved one who really wants you to succeed.

9. *Challenge Yourself—beat those numbers!*

    When it comes to our body, society has turned us into wimps by telling us we are at the mercy of our body. For example, if you have a cold, society has pontificated for eons to take it easy and rest. If you don't have a fever there is no reason to take it easy. Go do your workout. Of course, you need to be in touch with your body and listen when it says enough is enough, don't injure it. But also keep in mind that in order to excel at anything, you need to constantly challenge yourself. The same goes for your body. Great athletes always push their bodies past any and all barriers.

    A fun way to challenge yourself is to manage your exercise routine by numbers. It's exhilarating to beat your previous best. Create a daily log and write down a few key stats. Below are a few examples:

    a. While doing cardio keep track of your average heart rate and the number of calories burned at the twenty-minute mark. Then each day push yourself to beat the previous day's number by just a little.

b. If you bench pressed 155 pounds for the first time—congratulations for attaining your goal—now change your goal to 160 pounds and make it happen again.

c. Your weight training routine consisted of one set per exercise this entire month—next month increase it to two sets per exercise.

10. *Change your exercise routine frequently*

    If you do the same thing every day you will eventually get bored and burnout. Change it up!

Ten Tips to Help You Manage Your Meal Intake

The English language should abolish the word diet. Diets are mostly short-term solutions. The majority of people who diet eventually put the weight back on. Unfortunately, there are so many books written about various types of diets it has brainwashed much of the population. The most effective way to maintain the ideal weight is to manage your daily food intake. Below are ten tips to help you manage what you eat.

1. *Keep things simple*

   You don't need to count calories or follow a special diet. No one has time for that! Instead, weigh yourself daily. If you consume too many calories on any given day the scale will reflect this the next day. When this occurs, just eat a little less the next day or two. It's a simple way to manage your weight when you're always on the go.

2. *Establish phrases—play mind games*

   Train your mind to believe that managing your food intake is an integral part of your life. Use negative phrases or positive affirmations/techniques to train your mind (see Chapter One).

Repeatedly tell yourself the following negative phrases:

a. You look pathetic, can you imagine yourself in a bathing suit.
b. You're a fat slob.
c. You're so out of shape, you will probably die at a young age.
d. Get your lazy butt off that couch and clean your home.

Utilize the following techniques for positive reactions:

a. Tell yourself, "Your body is strong and healthy because you choose the right foods to keep it so."
b. Get a photo of a body you would like to have and look at it every day.
c. Practice stress techniques like yoga and meditation to stop comfort eating.
d. Partner up with someone who needs to get healthy and encourages you.
e. Remind yourself that a person's ability to accomplish something is only limited by their own self-doubt.

3. *Exercise will help curve your appetite*

   You already know that exercise burns calories, but did you know that after intense cardio workouts your appetite is curbed and you eat fewer calories throughout the day. There are many sources on the Internet supporting this fact. Although it's a temporary appetite suppression, some people find that exercising makes them reconsider their food choices. For instance, you might feel less inclined to chow down on pizza or hot wings after completing an afternoon run or morning step class, choosing a veggie sandwich or fruit smoothie instead.

4. *Drink water*

    Drinking water before meals can result in consuming less calories according to numerous studies. Your stomach will send signals to your brain that it's not hungry. It's zero calories, healthy and it will make you feel full. It doesn't get any easier than that. Drinking plenty of water also boosts your metabolism.

5. *Use smaller dishes and utensils*

    If you're overweight and have a tendency to over-eat, use smaller dishes and utensils. If you're constantly using large plates, you will be more inclined to fill it up with food, therefore consuming more calories. If you're using smaller plates and utensils, it will help you achieve portion control.

6. *Wear form-fitting clothes*

    I'm not suggesting you wear pants that are too tight, but when your clothes get noticeably tighter it may stop you from having a second helping of food. Especially as it can get expensive if you must repeatedly buy nice clothes to cover your growing waistline.

7. *Chew gum*

    If you're hungry and don't want to snack prior to dinner, try chewing gum to suppress your appetite. It really does work. Also, remember to chew slowly as it will help you lose weight.

8. *Don't snack from a bag or container*

   Put a small amount on your plate versus just snacking from the bag and not knowing the amount you're actually eating. You can divide the servings (noted on the label) into small baggies, but that's a lot of work. Just take a small handful out of the container and put the container away.

9. *Maintain a balanced diet—the five food groups*

   The five main food groups are dairy, fruits, grains, proteins and vegetables. They all provide vital nutrients to support normal healthy development. Choose foods that have a high content of nutrients (protein, vitamins, and minerals) compared with the number of calories, fat, and sodium content. Below are a few important tips:

   a. *Eat* fruits

      Like apples and berries, (especially strawberries and blueberries) which are a good source of fiber among other nutrients.

   b. *Eat more vegetables*

      Not only are they an excellent source of nutrients, but they're a good way to compliment your meal and help satisfy your hunger with minimal calories.

   c. *Eat lean proteins*

      Like low-fat yogurt and egg whites, especially in the morning, to help you feel fuller throughout the day. Aim for one ounce or thirty grams of protein per sitting, especially if you exercise daily. Also, if you exercise in the morning, you need to feed your muscles as quickly as possible post workout.

d. *Eat smaller portions and fewer carbohydrates*
It's all about strict maintenance of your carbohydrate intake (breads, pasta, potatoes and rice) as well as portion control (total number of calories consumed).

10. *Eat slowly to reduce calorie intake*
Eating slowly will help you consume fewer calories. Your food intake and appetite are controlled by hormones. After you eat, your stomach satisfies a hormone called ghrelin, which manages hunger. This hormone tells your mind that you've eaten, making you feel full, which helps you to stop eating. This process takes approximately twenty minutes, so slowing down when you eat gives your brain the time it needs to receive these signals. If you chow your meal down quickly, you will overeat as your brain doesn't have enough time to receive the 'I'm satisfied' signal.

Conclusion—Let's Toast—to a Healthier and Happier YOU

What a feeling . . . to be in shape, energetic and having the ability to live life to the fullest! There is *no* greater sensation. Adopting a healthy lifestyle doesn't have to be laborious, painful and/or mundane. Although it is an effort, we all know that the benefits far outweigh the challenges.

Living a healthy lifestyle needs to be a priority not a part-time effort. There is *no* middle ground. Either you make it habitual (daily routine/focus) or continue to struggle with your health-related challenges and lack of productivity. But, why wouldn't you make health a priority? It's mind-boggling that most individuals put it on the back-burner until there's a dire issue and they are forced to make health number one. Follow my health tips above and you'll love the new healthier you, waking up with a purpose each morning and eager to tackle the day! Your productivity level will skyrocket. Buckle up and enjoy the ride!

If you adopt the principles in chapters one-nine then congratulations to a healthier, happier and more productive you! That's the good news, however it's only the beginning and the better news is that there is no ending.

In the next chapter you learn how to continuously strategize to always improve. There are always things you can do differently to become more efficient!

Chapter 10

Continuously Strategize

You Can Always Do Better!

• • • And the last Principle, but certainly not least in importance is to continuously strategize to improve. You can always do better! Keep those wheels spinning . . . it's important to find new methods and techniques to be more efficient. As the demands on your time increase you need to be more productive than ever before! It's important to never stop growing personally and professionally.

What will it take to be more efficient and accomplish more to get the most out of your existence on this planet and to solidify your legacy? Perhaps it's changing your morning routine or perhaps it's getting to bed promptly in order to get ample sleep to be well-rested in the morning. Don't stop there. Which activities associated with life's most important priorities will help you achieve success faster? Since excelling in my Information Technology (IT) career (as quickly as possible) was one of my top priorities throughout my adult life, I was always strategizing on how to get to the top of my field and make the big bucks:

- How can I perform my job function more efficiently?
- How can I complete my projects ahead of schedule?
- Although my department doesn't have a training budget, how can I acquire the skills I need?
- How can I get promoted into a more senior position or even into management where the big bucks are?
- How can I get on management's radar and get noticed regularly for outstanding performance without making it too obvious?
- How can I spend more time networking and schmoozing with key staff/management at work?

Maintaining good health is everyone's priority, how can you improve your health regimen? What criteria can you monitor, assess and rate on a daily basis that would promote a healthy lifestyle? Perhaps it's what you eat that day and the quality of your exercise routine. My exercise routine is crucial to get my day started off on the right track. It begins each morning sometime between 4:00 and 5:30 AM and lasts approximately an hour and fifteen minutes. A good workout would mean:

- I felt mentally strong throughout my entire routine
- My legs felt strong during my cardiovascular workout and I burned 225 or more calories in twenty minutes and my average heart rate was always over 130
- I stretched
- I was very focused—there were no distractions

- I left the gym with a good (muscular) pump and a great attitude
- I had no injuries

Pick the indicators and categories that are the most relevant for your success and strategize to see where you can make improvements. Ask yourself constantly what will it take to:

- Accomplish your tasks and obligations more efficiently
- Stay focused on your goals and do everything possible to complete them ahead of schedule
- Ensure that you maintain balance in the four main priorities of life, which includes not overlooking your relationship obligations

Never settle! You will never be perfect but never stop trying to seek perfection! Strategize every chance you get; when you're in a long traffic jam, waiting for your haircut appointment, or perhaps you're watching a movie with your family that is boring, but your presence is important look at the screen but utilize your mind to strategize, etc.

Besides, You Will Never Be Satisfied—Enjoy the Feeling

As you're Building the Best Version of You, and taste the feeling of continuous accomplishments, you will never be satisfied. You will ALWAYS want more. Life is all about accomplishments: The more you accomplish, one thing after another, the happier you become. What a rush, like no other feeling. Those are real highs. It's a self-inflicted adrenaline rush you can't get out of your system once you've experienced it. The more you accomplish, the more you crave accomplishments for yourself. Now that you've built the best version of you, you will never be satisfied. What a feeling it is to always want more, take on new challenges and accomplish more year after year. Life now has purpose. The only way to accomplish more is to continue to improve your efficiency.

I can't imagine not accomplishing one goal after another until the day I drop. If there are no accomplishments, there is no life, or at best, it's an unfulfilled life. There is no purpose for living. You may exist, but that's not living. Living is progressing, not merely breathing.

"To live is so startling it leaves little time for anything else."
—Emily Dickinson

The true measure of a person's success and happiness is their emotional, physical and psychological well-being. Never be satisfied with the level of success and happiness you've attained. There are always areas in our lives that need attention to keep the balance consistent. Being happy in all aspects of your life is the mother of all accomplishments. Don't settle. If you must, remember to always settle for more.

Strategize on How to Minimize or Better Yet Eliminate Those Bad Days

When you have a re-occurring issue—confront it. Stop brushing it aside or masking negative emotions. Keep it in the forefront and use that pent-up frustration to motivate yourself to light a fire under your butt and strategize to create permanent solutions. What's the point of telling yourself: There, there . . . it's okay or tomorrow will be a brighter day unless those words hold some weight? Right now, those words are meaningless. We all have those negative days where nothing goes your way. How do you minimize those bad days or at the very least don't repeat the same issues that caused that negativity in the first place? Below is a synopsis of what transpired with one of my clients who was trying to deal with the same negative issue for over a year. Instead of tackling the issue head-on she would brush it aside.

> *Her boss was not very people-oriented and oftentimes rude. At least once a week she would go home in a foul mood, which severely impacted the quality of her sleep. Unfortunately, she had to interact with him. When she woke up the next morning, she pretended like nothing was wrong and that today was another beautiful day — woohoo I'm going to remain positive. Remaining positive is a good thing but it doesn't fix the issue.*
>
> *While at work she performed at a superior level and went out of her way to try and please her boss—hoping that he would eventually change his nasty disposition, but all to no avail. Instead of wasting cycles wondering whether or not he would ever be nice, strategize to fix your predicament. Perhaps assess other organizations and their opportunities, sharpen your skills, network to meet key individuals, keep your resume updated and actively look for new employment—just in case. Keep him in the forefront and remember who he is and what he is and that you cannot change him but you can minimize those bad hair days by continuously strategizing to fix your predicament.*

Negativity is not always a bad thing—use it to your advantage—you have the power to fix things! Be proactive with your life. Fix the areas that are broken or cause you grief.

Grade Your Performance DAILY

With approximately half of my clients, I recommend that they monitor and document their performance daily to gauge their overall effectiveness. I mention it to only half because there is additional overhead involved and many of my clients already struggle with administrative responsibilities. In other words, they would push it aside and only do it when it was absolutely necessary. Unfortunately, this causes other problems i.e., bills are misplaced or paid late, paperwork not filed properly when it's time to do taxes, etc. But for others who want to see how well they performed by the numbers; I recommend the following method: On a scale to ten (where ten is highly efficient), rate your overall productivity. How did your performance impact your priorities today? It's important to critique every aspect of your day starting from the time you got out of bed to the time you go to sleep. Did you get out of bed promptly and with passion to attack your priorities? Did you operate with urgency throughout the entire day/evening? Did you have a quality workout? If you started getting tired in the afternoon, did you slow down and comply or did you do something to combat your fatigue? What about your evening routine—did you stay disciplined? Did you select your clothes for the next day? Did you prepare your to-do list for tomorrow? Did you go to bed at a decent hour?

Most of you will always have more to do than hours in a day, so doesn't it make sense to get the biggest bang for the buck? And what better way to begin that process than to gauge your efficiency for the sixteen hours you're awake?

Below is an actual spreadsheet from one of my clients. His priorities were his

- Finances: To earn more and cut back on expenditures
- Health: exercise every morning prior to leaving for work
- Business: grow it bigtime.

We put a maximum weight factor for each one of his priorities plus overall discipline:

- Finances: 2
- Health: 2
- Business: 2
- Overall discipline: 4

Below is a seven-day snapshot of the spreadsheet I used to track his performance during the mentoring phase. Each evening along with sending me a copy of his to-do list for the next day, he would email me a recap rating his performance.

Date	Priority	Productivity	Notes
4/22/19	Finances	1	Spent 28.00 on breakfast (way too much)
	Health	2	Good workout
	Business	2	Focused on high priority business related tasks
	Discipline	2	Woke up 20 minutes late
		7	

Building the Best Version of You

Date	Priority	Productivity	Notes
4/23/19	Finances	2	Stayed in budget and proactively checked all accounts
	Health	1	Only exercised for ten minutes
	Business	1	Was distracted throughout the day on lower-level tasks
	Discipline	1	Not very efficient today
		5	
4/24/19	Finances	1	Went out to lunch and spent too much
	Health	0	Did not meal prep - ate junk food all day
	Business	1	Not focused all day
	Discipline	1	Not an efficient day
		3	
4/25/19	Finances	2	Stayed in budget
	Health	0	Did not exercise
	Business	1	Did the bare minimum
	Discipline	0	Wasted one hour on phone with sister listening to her drama, did not do admin tasks, woke up late
		3	
4/26/19	Finances	2	Stayed in budget
	Health	1	Couldn't finish workout in the morning
	Business	2	Very focused
	Discipline	3	Angered by lame workout - pushed hard remainder of the day
		8	

Date	Priority	Productivity	Notes
4/27/19	Finances	2	Stayed in budget
	Health	2	Solid workout
	Business	0	I wasn't productive enough with my programming - couldn't complete high priority: code review for the day
	Discipline	3	Good day
		7	
4/28/19	Finances	2	Proactively monitored all accounts and
	Health	2	I ate well and had a solid workout
	Business	2	I was productive with all of my high priority business related tasks
	Discipline	4	Great day
		10	

As you can see, he had some good days and some really bad days early in his development. It's important to assess your performance, strategize, make adjustments and continue to move forward. One of the most effective ways to continue to grow is by monitoring, assessing and rating your progress daily. It only takes a few minutes. The rewards can be substantial. It's not enough to be productive occasionally, you need to seek perfection every day.

You will never be perfect but never stop trying to seek perfection!

Conclusion—Status Quo is Failure

What's the point of going through an entire lifetime doing the same things, with the same outcomes, never growing as a human being and not accomplishing your major goals? If you define life as: Getting up around 7:00 PM, going to work, coming home at 6:00 PM, watching TV for a few hours, and going to sleep—in other words, the same old boring routine Monday—Friday then your current lifestyle is failure in my book. If complacency is your cup of tea, then, your current lifestyle is a waste of your livelihood. You are capable of getting so much more out of life and I'm sure you don't need me to tell you that. Continue to exist or LIVE!

If you need further assistance on how to strategize to make the most out of your life, I am offering 45 minutes of complimentary consultation via telephone: 818.404.9248, Skype, WhatsApp, FaceTime or you can meet with me in person if you live near my homes in Frisco, Texas or Fort Lauderdale, Florida. You can also email me at harris@harriskern.com.

Epilogue

If I was to encapsulate what this book is all about, it would be:

> *The strategy to achieve your goals, the discipline to hold yourself accountable and the EQ to manage your emotions.*

I am Human—I will Never be Perfect—but I did Pretty Good

I did an okay job abiding by the spiritual Ten Commandments all of my adult life—I would probably grade myself a B-. Nothing to be proud about, but at least I didn't break any laws. I have practiced the *Ten Principles* I pontificate throughout this book for over four decades—I would probably grade myself a A-. In the early years of my personal and professional development I deviated and experimented, I even put more emphasis on my favorite *Principles* and totally ignored others. My mentor warned me early on to stay grounded—keep true to your values (your ego will grow as your net worth expands). He also told me to adhere to all *Ten Principles* equally and practice them religiously in all four key areas of life, which I discuss throughout the book.

I didn't heed his warning because of a super enlarged ego and the hunger for more material, excitement and power. Although I became rich, successful and had name recognition in my career, I slowly transitioned into a downright pathetic human being and it all came crashing down! I fell (hard) several times and I deserved each fall, I lost many of those material possessions I craved.

It took some time, but I came back from the bowels of hell to be happy once again and I owe it all to being disciplined, learning how to manage my emotions (graduated with honors from the school of EQ), and my relationship with God! So, I decided to inscribe them as the *Ten Principles for Success and Happiness* and along with *fully* adhering to the spiritual Ten Commandments made for a pretty good life in the end.

Will I ever make another mistake again? I'm sure I will, but I'm also certain that I will learn from my mistakes and continue to grow until I take my last breath on this planet.

Whenever you slip-up, don't get too hard on yourself, tell yourself: "I've progressed so much to date and no one is perfect" and move on, don't dwell on what you did wrong. And who cares what anyone else thinks, you know who you are—and as long as you stay the course and follow both sets of values—go make it happen!

Oh, What a Feeling—Taking Control of Your Life

You will actually feel superhuman. That may sound like an exaggeration, but it's how I actually feel every day. I'm on top of the world—bring it on! I have taken control of my life and it feels incredible. What does it mean to take control of your life? Is it possessing self-discipline to accomplish all of your goals? Is it the ability to influence your fate? Is it being able to manage your current lifestyle? Is it the ability to remain positive, regardless of the negativity surrounding you occasionally? Is it the wherewithal to be motivated to operate a high-level every day of the year? Is it the means to manage your emotions? It's all of the above and building a herculean level of self-confidence while focusing on your priorities along this great journey.

I have the confidence to take it all on and then some. I am not being arrogant —just being very confident in my capabilities. To accomplish *every* one of your goals is a feeling that's second to none, especially those major goals! If you can adopt all *Ten Principles* you will master your life and according to my maturity model. You will:

- Live life with a sense of urgency
- Constantly be motivated
- Redirect negative emotions into a powerful positive force of energy
- Possess a *never* enough mentality
- Be intolerant of failing the war—although you may lose some battles
- Constantly put pressure on yourself to produce at a higher level—no outside pressure or obstacle will stress you out
- You will not take a long fall after a major breakup with your partner or any other emotional turmoil
- Be energetic
- Maintain values
- Live a balanced lifestyle
- Be happy

When I achieved self-mastery and built a pretty darn-good version of myself, I knew it. I was different internally. Outwardly, I portrayed the same happy-go-lucky demeanor, but internally I was 'robotic-like'. I was operating at high intensity every day. Please do not take this the wrong way. Although I was machine-like with my actions, I never pushed my new-found sense of urgency on anyone else. Actually no one knew there was a difference except for my friends who noticed I was accomplishing things at lightning speed. I was in one mode *every* day. I was on a mission. My mission was to accomplish, accomplish and accomplish more. One accomplishment or several accomplishments meant very little. Sure, I was excited—maybe for a few minutes or an hour, but then it was on to another goal and eventually another accomplishment. Your mind will act as a guiding, calculating tool that will provide you with continuous immense benefits.

Once you achieve self-mastery, you will always want more: to be healthier, own more property, go on more vacations and help more people than ever before. You won't be able to stop—enjoy the permanent and continuous high.

It's all about that Legacy

One of my most important goals in life was to leave behind a legacy of accomplishments. If I cross the street tomorrow and get run over by a truck, it's not enough that the people I've mentored (especially my children) will have something for the rest of their lives to remember me by. It's not enough that I've made them productive or that I've helped them to help themselves become successful. *I want more!* I want to have a major impact on people that I've never met before. I want to be remembered by many accomplishments so individuals can emulate via one word and that's *discipline. Discipline is the defining element in your life. With it you can achieve almost anything; without it, you struggle to exist.* I want them to turn to *discipline* now, and even when I'm long gone. My ultimate goal is to have my name associated with *discipline* so others can achieve self-mastery.

—***Harris Kern***

About the Authors

Harris Kern

Harris Kern is one of the world's leading organization and personal mentors (www.disciplinementor.com). He is a frequent speaker and seminar leader at business and management conferences. His passion is to help people excel in their professional and personal life by developing their self-discipline skills to combat the top issues: severe procrastination, poor time management, ineffective goal management, lack of focus, no sense of urgency and poor motivation. He also helps individuals improve their EQ skills (managing emotions, relationship management, communication, etc.) and leadership skills. Mr. Kern is also the author of over forty books. Some of the titles include:

- *Going from Undisciplined to Self-Mastery: Five Simple Steps to Get You There*
- *On Being a Workaholic: Using Balance and Discipline to live a Better and More Efficient Life*
- *Live Like You Are Dying: Making Your Life Count Moment by Moment*
- *DISCIPLINE: Six Steps to Unleashing Your Hidden Potential*

- *DISCIPLINE: Training the Mind to Manage Your Life*
- *DISCIPLINE: Take Control of Your Life*

Mr. Kern is recognized as the foremost authority on practical guidance for solving management issues and challenges. He has devoted over thirty years helping professionals build competitive organizations. His client list reads like a who's who of American and international business. His client list includes Standard and Poor's, GE, The Weather Channel, News Corporation, Hong Kong Air Cargo Terminal (HACTL) and hundreds of other Fortune 500 and Global 2000 companies.

Mr. Kern is the founder and driving force behind the Enterprise Computing Institute (www.harriskern.com) and the best-selling series of books published by Prentice Hall. As founder of the Enterprise Computing Institute, he has brought together the industry's leading minds to publish how-to textbooks on the critical issues the IT industry faces. The series includes titles such as:

- IT Services
- CIO Wisdom
- CIO Wisdom II
- Managing IT as an Investment

Mr. Kern's goal is to arm individuals and organizations with the tools to empower them to become more productive and successful.

More than Forty Years of Being Productive and Successful

Mr. Kern lives every day with a sense of urgency! Life is short and he makes use of every minute NOT hour or day! Mr. Kern pushes himself extremely hard (by choice):

- Exercises every day of the year
- Has traveled to every continent (except Antarctica) and hundreds of cities all over the world (some several times)
- Has established several successful businesses
- Purchased first home at the age of nineteen in the San Francisco Bay Area
- Trained his mind and body to sleep four hours a night
- Financially set at the age of thirty-eight

Most people would consider his routine crazy and unhealthy; however, Mr. Kern is 66 years old and he has mastered the ultimate level of discipline since his early twenties. Mr. Kern believes that the body and mind should be pushed to the max every single day. The difference is he has the experience to do so; however, Mr. Kern would never push his clients in this manner unless, of course, this is their wish.

Mr. Kern's greatest assets are his caring demeanor, incomparable energy, and desire to help people manage their life efficiently. He wants to help as many people as possible fulfill their goals and aspirations.

Thank you

Dear A'ishah, thank you for agreeing to be my partner on this book. You are like a daughter to me and I am grateful to have you in my life.

A'ishah Khan

A'ishah Khan is an author and speaker driven by a heart-felt belief that human connection is the key to making the world a better place. Her writing style evokes strong emotions in her readers, thanks to her innate ability to connect with the experiences of others. Described as a 'velvet brick', her message hits home hard with the softest of intentions. A'ishah's love of life can be warmly felt; a nurturing demeanor underscored with a strength brought about by her life experiences. With a curious mind that never rests, she has worked for more than ten years as a pharmacist, writer, and public speaker, contributing to the conversation around mental health and well-being in many ways.

Her journey as a writer has been an indirect one. Known for her deep empathy, attention to detail, and skillful communication, A'ishah has been a lifelong wordsmith creating other worlds and characters from the early age of three. A first generation American of Indian descent, she learned to read and write Urdu, Arabic and English as a toddler. Despite her love of language and earning multiple recognitions throughout her life, she decided to forgo writing and pursued the security of a career in pharmacy.

After earning her doctorate in pharmacy from the University of Florida in 2007, she completed a residency at the James A. Haley VA Hospital. Here, she helped pioneer clinical pharmacy as the first pharmacist in charge of the 40-bed inpatient psychiatry unit. She also earned her Core Coaching and Mentoring Certification, along with training in TEACH principles and leadership classes. While she was able to maintain her love of writing through involvement in numerous pharmacy policies, articles, and journals, it was never quite enough.

A'ishah then faced health difficulties, which led her on a path of self-discovery. Despite being a pharmacist, she learned to live naturally, healing her body, mind and soul with elements from the earth rather than man-made medications. This journey to newfound health revived her and brought her back to what she loves; writing. During this period of intense transformation, A'ishah's mission as an author was born; to strike a chord in the hearts of her readers—like the mesmerizing melody of a song—to make heard even the hardest of messages. This book is the culmination of this powerful transformation. She is now also working on her own coming-of-age fiction novel.

Along with her continued work as a clinical pharmacist specializing in mental health, A'ishah strives to use her voice for the betterment of others. Completing a journalism internship with a local news channel, she has brought her passion for writing together with her desire to impact lives through storytelling. She has presented national lectures on evidence-based strategies to support veterans with PTSD and explored integrative care through collaborations between physicians, pharmacists and psychologists. Her philanthropic efforts have also successfully raised over $100,000 for the construction of a state-of-the-art orphanage in Mali, Africa.

Beyond her career pursuits, A'ishah loves spending time with family, photography, and traveling the world. She has a taste for adventure, from simple hiking and kayaking to the more thrilling bungee jumping, parasailing and sand surfing! With a strong belief that life is full of infinite possibilities, she lives by the quote from her favorite movie *Back to the Future*, "Your future hasn't been written yet. No one's has ... So, make it a good one."

Thank you

Thank you . . . first and foremost to God, my motivation to strive for excellence—when I was lost—You guided me.

To my partner in crime, HK, you saw my potential and pushed me to a level of excellence similar to yours. Attached to the hip, through all the nonsense you became like a father-figure to me. I know I tested your patience at times, but you never lost your calm. Your depth of caring is unmatched . . . a true diamond in the rough. Thank you for all the good times and for allowing me the honor of being your co-author.

To my family, you know who you are, you believed in me when I failed to believe in myself. And lastly, to my gift from God, may this book be a reminder that angels do exist.

Ever faithful, ever patient, A'ishah.

www.ingramcontent.com/pod-product-compliance
Lightning Source LLC
Chambersburg PA
CBHW030904080526
44589CB00010B/140